MW01200878

Understanding
Bob Dylan

Making Sense of the Songs That Changed Modern Music

Tony Beck

ISBN: 1461147816
ISBN-13: 9781461147817
LCCN: 2011909061

TABLE OF CONTENTS

ACKNOWLEDGEMENTS

This book's been a long time coming. It wouldn't have happened without Joanne Sandler and Mitch Blank. Comments on individual chapters were gratefully received from Paul Beck, David Beaver, who pointed out that sometimes Dylan uses rhymes because they sound good, Richard Thomson, Peter Busby, Julie Emerson, John Mitchell, Jonathan Beckitt, and Erin Nichols. Thanks are due to Roya Nasser for suggestions on marketing. Books by Christopher Ricks, Stephen Scobie and Michael Gray were inspirational.

Gratitude is due to Jeff Rosen at Special Rider Music for the kind permission to quote from Bob Dylan's songs. I hope the book reflects that trust. Other permissions are duly noted at the end of the book.

Aaron and Hannah gave me all the support I could wish for, and then some.

Margie faced multiple readings and listenings – on the Eurostar, on flights to London, in the lands of the rainforest and the hills – and endured them all with grace; gave me lots of ideas, and even became something of a Dylan fan.

Royalties from this book will be donated to Sahanivasa, a society fighting against poverty and untouchability in Southern India, with whom I have had the honour of working.

This book is dedicated to my Mum and Dad. My Mum didn't live to see it, but my Dad made it through.

CHAPTER 1

Introduction: welcome to Dyland

My first memory of Bob Dylan was my brother playing a vinyl copy of "Blonde on Blonde". It must have been 1969, because around that time Paul took me to an anti-Vietnam war protest at the US embassy in Grosvenor Square, London, and filmed the crowds while standing on top of a red London mail box, until told to get down by the cops. That blurry photograph of Dylan on the cover of "Blonde on Blonde", the slurred singing and weird imagery, and the awakening of political consciousness, are all there in my imagination.

Ten years later I'm writing an undergraduate thesis on "Blood on the Tracks" as part of the requirement to complete a BA in English Literature. I can still hear the sounds of my old typewriter, as the click clack clacking of the keys echoed across the courtyard from the room where I stayed up nights typing. The supervisor for that thesis gave me about 30 vinyl bootlegs to record, and I spent a week putting them on tape, listening to the endless drone of early

Dylan. In 1978 I drove to Blackbushe south of London with my then girlfriend and we swung to "Changing of the Guards" with 200,000 or so others.

Forward to 2006. Like many early fans, I hadn't listened to Dylan in almost 20 years. He comes to Vancouver, Canada (where I live) and after a noisy concert stands on stage for a couple of minutes with his hands slightly raised to acknowledge fans who have followed him for so long. Nice gesture. Scorsese releases the movie "No Direction Home", and Dylan is for the most part unintelligible. A friend in New York tells me about a collector who has all Dylan's recordings since 1956, plus original hand written lyrics, and many other things, and who worked on the Scorsese movie. I'm uninterested at first, but then read the first volume of Dylan's autobiography "Chronicles" and "Dylan's Visions of Sin", by my old Prof., Christopher Ricks. There's an exhibition of Dylan's early years at the Morgan Library in New York, and I visit one late rainy November evening to find the room packed with young people. Soon I'm sitting in Greenwich Village with the archivist with the original handwritten lyrics to "Blood on the Tracks" in front of me – an extraordinary experience to see in Dylan's scrawl and revisions the fury behind the creation of those songs. And as we'll see in Chapter 2, on love and money, Dylan's notebook for "Blood on the Tracks" provides insights into the way in which he uses one of the oldest literary traditions.

I start listening and thinking about Dylan again and .....doors and windows.

You will search, babe

How are we to understand Dylan's work, the codes, pictures and messages of the songs, and why they mean so much to so many? These are the questions this book seeks to answer. The point of this book is to figure out how Dylan has used particular literary and musical themes and traditions to fashion extraordinary songs. He draws on, changes, falls foul of, and advances those traditions – from the English romantic poets, to Walt Whitman, to Woody Guthrie and Hank Williams, to Joseph Conrad.

The idea is not to track down Dylan's sources, which Ricks, Polito, Gray and others have done so well[1], but to understand his work as a whole. Now that Dylan's work is getting close to complete in terms of creative writing (barring any viagra-like musical renaissance), it's possible to look at the themes that permeate his work, the symbols and images that are repeated, and which structure and bind his songs into a remarkably coherent whole. As Dylan said: "songs need structure, stratagems, codes and

---

[1]   Christopher Ricks (2005) *Dylan's Visions of Sin* New York: ECCO. Michael Gray (2004) *Song and Dance Man III* London: Continuum; Robert Polito "Bob Dylan: Henry Nimrod Revisited". http://www.poetryfoundation.org/archive/feature.html?id=178703; Thomas, R. (2007) "The Streets of Rome: The Classical Dylan." In *Oral Tradition* 22 (1). Because Dylan has drawn from a wide range of sources does not necessarily mean that the resulting songs are of high quality, a point made by Clive James "Bringing some of it all back home", in B. Hedin (2004)(ed) *The Bob Dylan Reader: Studio A* New York: Norton and Company, pp. 98-108.

stability."[2] Despite the multiple changes in musical direction over almost 50 years, and some would say the multiple changes in persona, there is a remarkable consistency to the themes on which he dwells. Some themes such as the highway and road permeate every aspect of his songs – no surprise perhaps given his well-recorded debt to the blues. Others may surprise more, such as his attitude towards creativity. The themes and traditions I explore are those around which Dylan organizes his songs – love, sex and money and ambivalence about love; his attitude towards writing and creating; his use of the highway and the romantic traveler and outsider, the individual against society, and his use of boundaries; and the way he writes about time and memory.

I look at these themes and traditions as "common poetic denominators" – common symbols to most writers, and which we instantly recognise when we hear Dylan's songs, if only unconsciously. These common symbols carry with them the weight of literary history, and each has multiple meanings, and it's from here they get much of their intensity. But the writer needs to be careful, because ill or over use of these symbols can simply be corny and hackneyed.

Here's one of many examples of common poetic denominators – broad literary themes that have structured much of modern western literature - I look at in this book, from the 1974/5 song on "Blood on the Tracks", "You're a Big Girl Now".

---

2   Quoted in Ricks, p. 353.

Bird on the horizon, sittin' on a fence,
He's singin' his song for me at his own expense.
And I'm just like that bird, oh, oh,
Singin' just for you.

Dylan is drawing in these lines on multiple themes in western literature, and also referring to his own work on "Blood on the Tracks" and before. First is the singing bird - so common on "Blood on the Tracks" that there is a singing (or talking) bird on almost every one of those bloody tracks, but also the many other birds in his songs, from the rooster crowing in "Don't Think Twice It's Alright", and the white dove in "Blowin' in the Wind". He is also making the comparison between the bird and the singer/poet - "I'm just like that bird"- which so many writers have used. Then there is the bird on the horizon, on the fence, the boundary which needs to be followed or transcended along with so many other boundaries such as tracks, lines, roads, and highways which criss-cross Dylan's songs in a highly ambivalent way. Third comes the pain of singing and of creation - "at his own expense" – literally the cost of singing, or paying dues in "Tangled up in Blue", and the tension between love and money that forms such an important part of "Blood on the Tracks", Dylan's work, and western literature. It's the compression of so much into four seemingly simple lines, but also the borrowing from themes in much of modern western literature, that give Dylan's words so much power. This book returns often to the lyrics of "Blood on the Tracks", because it's here that the themes that structure Dylan's work are most intense.

Dylan's use of language is often so purposefully vague that his lyrics are inevitably subject to multiple interpretations. And his is such a rich body of work that there are many other themes in his work – identity, personal responsibility and death being three which others have uncovered, but..... this is my take on Bob Dylan. Many artists dwell possessively on themes and images to try and make sense of and put some order in their world – the American/European tension in Henry James, the tower and the gyre in Yeats, obsession in Dostoevsky, the pain and pleasure of love, the despair about the lost muse.

There are four main kinds of writing about Dylan. There are the numerous autobiographies, picture and photograph books that remind us that, after all, Dylan is a rock star who been around for 50 years, has sold a phenomenal number of records, and still has a rock star's following – in that we're interested if he falls out of a tree or owns ten houses; and which, on a slightly more serious level, attempts to make connections between his life and his songs. Second there are writers like Greil Marcus who like to write about Dylan but in fact are creating their own (in Marcus' case very entertaining) fiction, using Dylan and his songs as the starting point for their creative process, almost like a poet using another poet as the subject for a poem, as Seamus Heaney does in his poem "Elegy" on Robert Lowell.. Then there is the third kind already alluded to, the Dylan Detectives, who try to make sense of his songs by searching for his sources, a game Dylan has himself fuelled recently by drawing on more and more obscure works, knowing someone will eventually track him down. Fourth there are the literary critics such as Scobie, Ricks and Gray who situate Dylan's work in the broader context of English and other literatures, and into which category I am hoping this book will fall.

First warning: there isn't much biography here. Dylan's life has been trawled over like the innards of an animal, looking for portents and signs.[3] His marriages, his early days in New York, his religion, how many houses he owns, are all ..... overdone. It's key to recognise that even though many of Dylan's songs may seem personal or confessional, just because he or any other writer writes in the first person does not mean they are referring to their own experience. When Bruce Springsteen writes through the eyes of a firefighter in "The Rising", or Robert Browning writes in the form of dramatic monologue, we don't assume that they are writing about their personal experience, we assume the opposite, that they have taken on someone else's persona for the purposes of the song or poem. When Dylan writes in "Sweetheart Like You"[4]:

You know, a woman like you should be at home,
That's where you belong,

---

3 Howard Sounes in *Down the Highway*, (Grove Press, 2001) has done the most thorough trawling to date.

4 All the lyrics quoted in this book are taken from the website: http://www.bobdylan.com/index.html

There is an extensive discussion of the changing nature of Dylan's songs in performance in Stephen Scobie's (2003) *Alias Bob Dylan Revisited*. Calgary: Red Deer Press. As Scobie notes (p. 110): "For Dylan there is no definitive text." I don't deal with this issue much, but where particular changes to songs are relevant for my discussion they are noted.

Watching out for someone who loves you true
Who would never do you wrong.
Just how much abuse will you be able to take?
Well, there's no way to tell by that first kiss.
What's a sweetheart like you doin' in a dump like this?

Is he really expressing the opinion that women should be at home and possibly be abused, or is he putting into song what used to be and still is in some circles a common view about women? Dylan's songs about love are much more complex than the first interpretation of these lines would suggest, so should we give him the benefit of the doubt and say this is a song about a particular viewpoint, rather than Dylan's own viewpoint? Should we trust the singer or the song?

One of the most interesting things about Dylan is his devotion to his art; he is, above all, a songwriter and artist. As we'll see in Chapter 3, on writing and meta-fiction, he's fascinated by, and fearful of, the act of creation. His art transcends the individual experience, including his own, and creates something that is relevant to many. Even a song like "Sara" which would appear to be autobiographical because it's title is the name of Dylan's then wife, may have other wider literary references.[5]

Second warning, there's not a lot of comparison here in terms of Dylan being "great", or between Dylan's albums and songs. As Confucius never said, only

---

5   See Scobie, p. 281.

sorrow comes from comparing one thing with another. We all know Dylan has had an enormous influence on popular culture and other artists. He sings to the outsider in many of us. Ninety million albums sold, hundreds of songs, a couple of hundred books and thousands of articles about him, speak to his contributions to popular culture. Is he, like, in the top ten singers of all time, is "Like a Rolling Stone" the best song ever recorded, is he a better poet than Keats, is he better than Springsteen or the Beatles? A lot of people seem to care, but that's just our modern-day obsession with lists (a theme explored in chapter two), and doesn't help much in understanding his songs.

Third warning: I'm disinclined to believe much of what Dylan says in interviews, and there are few quotes in this book from the many interviews he has given. Dylan is a terrible interlocutor, but that's the point – in his interviews he cancels out the difficulty of not wanting to say anything but saying nothing, with varied inflection. Take this reported interview from February 1978 in Tokyo:

> *When asked the reason for his decision to visit Japan, Dylan offered no explanation. The reporters also asked Dylan to define the age that they lived in, to which Dylan replied, after some hesitation, that is was the "Zen age." When he was asked to elaborate, he conceded that he did not know much about Zen, expect that he had once read about it in a book.*[6]

6   Tachi, M. (2009) "Bob Dylan's Reception in Japan." In Sheehy, C. and T. Swiss (eds) *Highway 61 Revisited. Bob Dylan's Road from Minnesota to the World*. Minneapolis: University of Minneapolis Press, 117.

Or how about this one from an interview about his 2001 album " 'Love and Theft' " in *La Repubblica* that surfaced on the internet in 2006. When asked if he reads books on history, Dylan apparently said: "Not any more than would be natural to do." Good to hear that Dylan isn't into the unnatural reading of history books. He likes playing around in interviews and often appears to approach them like a game of identity hide and seek, offering brief glimpses and then disappearing behind a wall of jokes, impenetrable comments, or sentence structures that could have come straight out of a Jose Saramago novel and leave us a long time afterwards wondering if the words have any meaning. Perhaps that's what happens when you get asked the same questions hundreds of times. It's almost like an art form, and that's how the Morgan Library exhibit I mentioned treated it, replaying one of his more famous interviews continuously alongside the originals of some of his lyrics. He's also a great self-promoter, and there's nothing better than contradicting yourself for self-promotion and media attention. So let's trust the songs, and not the singer.

Fourth, I don't spend a lot of time writing about Dylan's music. That's better left to music critics (who know something about music) rather than literary critics. For Marshall, who does write about Dylan's music, this is one of the most problematic aspects of Dylan criticism:

> There is a problem, however, in treating Dylan as a poet, and that is the fact that he writes songs

rather than poems. although, at the start of their books, virtually all of the literary critics offer some kind of fleeting acknowledgement that Dylan's songs are sung rather than read, this is seldom acted upon and the result is an over-emphasis on Dylan's lyrics....songs gain their emotional and artistic power not merely from the semantic meaning of the lyrics but from a constellation of sound. Dylan's words are performed: music, voice, and words come together to create a distinctive artefact and not a verbalized poem. To analyze them effectively requires taking into account both the music and vocal performance.... If we are to understand the emotional affect and artistic content of Dylan's songs, utilizing the assumptions underpinning the literary approach to Dylan may lead us in the wrong direction, over-emphasizing semantic meaning rather than sonic experience. [7]

This may be true for individual songs, but not I would argue for Dylan's work as a whole. For example, Marshall uses "Sad-Eyed Lady of the Lowlands", released in 1966 on "Blonde on Blonde"[8] as a song with little meaning but where the music wraps up the words of the song "and gives them their meaning, lending them both grace and warmth. The lyrics don't stand up as poetry on a page, because they

---

7   Marshall, L. (2009) "Bob Dylan and the Academy". In Kevin Dettmar (ed) *The Cambridge Companion to Bob Dylan*. Cambridge: Cambridge University Press, pp. 100
8   Album names and dates of release are usually included for non-Dylanists.

don't have to." This is an unfortunate example, as I'll show in the next chapter, because "Sad-Eyed Lady of the Lowlands" not only draws together many images from "Blonde and Blonde", but also fits into a centuries old poetic tradition.

Come to think of it, Dylan has been pretty critical of critics who dissect his songs like rabbits. Well, tough luck, if you put your songs out there you have to expect people to talk about them. Some of the interpretations I've read have been pretty far-fetched, or at least I couldn't see the connections. But is Dylan, or any artist, aware of all the subtleties of their writing? Here is Ricks:

> So if I am asked whether I believe that Dylan is conscious of all the subtle effects of wording and timing that I suggest, I am perfectly happy to say that he probably isn't. And if I am right, then in this he is not less the artist, but more….T.S. Eliot knew…. that…"the poet does many things upon instinct, for which he can give no better account than anyone else."[9]

I'd agree with Ricks on this one. And looking for themes that dissect the work is perhaps the best way to approach this complex writer. Sometimes what we see and hear is Dylan's brilliance, but at

---

9   Ricks pp. 8-9.

other times perhaps it's the English language, like the night, playing tricks.

So, in this book we will make sense of Dylan's songs by figuring out how and why he uses certain literary traditions, starting with love, money and sex. If this intrigues, read on.

CHAPTER 2

Dylan, love, sex and money

With your mercury mouth in the missionary times,
And your eyes like smoke and your prayers like
rhymes,
And your silver cross, and your voice like chimes,
Oh, who among them do they think could bury
you?

So begins the puzzling, evocative, mesmeric "Sad-Eyed Lady of the Lowlands", the last track of "Blonde on Blonde" which Dylan released in 1966, a song that has caught many Dylanists in its head-lights. "Puzzling" - some would say meaningless - because this song contains weirdly complex imagery. "With your mercury mouth in the missionary times" – good luck working that one out. It's a song that has elicited fundamentally different views from admirers and critics – and sometimes the same person. Dylan encyclopaedist, and author of "Song and Dance Man" Michael Gray, hated the song, then loved it. First he wrote a damning two page criticism which concluded:

In the end, whatever the song's attractions and clever touches, they have been bundled together, and perhaps a bit complacently, without the unity either of a clear and real theme or of cohesive artistic discipline.

Later Gray recanted:

When I read this assessment now, I simply feel embarrassed at what a little snob I was when I wrote it. In contrast (and paradoxically), when I go back and listen, after a long gap, to Dylan's recording, every ardent, true feeling I ever had comes back to me. Decades of detritus drop away and I feel back in communion with my best self and my soul. Whatever the shortcomings of the lyric, the recording itself, capturing at its absolute peak Dylan's incomparable capacity for intensity of communication, is a masterpiece if ever there was one. It isn't like listening to a record: it enfolds you, to use a word from the song itself, in a whole universe.

Good for you, honest Michael! And that such an insightful critic can have such a different perspective on the same song shows how complex it is. Clive James denigrates[10]:

Dylan's unstable sense of organization is most readily noticeable in the long songs that don't

---

10   James, C. (2004) "Bringing Some of it All Back Home." In B. Hedin (ed) *The Bob Dylan Reader. Studio A.* New York: Norton, p. 106.

justify their length. "Sad-Eyed Lady of the Lowlands" is too obvious a case to bear examination – it would be a dunce indeed who imagined that in purchasing Blonde on Blonde he had got hold of much more than one and half LPs.

Marshall vilifies:

The lyrics to "Sad-Eyed Lady of the Lowlands" are vague and imprecise, with the potential to be dismissed as some of the worst excesses of Dylan's symbolist pretensions.[11]

Bangs disparages (who knew there were so many negative words out there?):

Another thing that might occur to you if you're willing to go this far into cynicism is that, if in the sixties we really were ready to accept absolutely any drivel that dropped out of his mouth – a mercury mouth in the missionary times, say…[12]

But Gray's reversal, and similarly strong opinions don't get us any nearer to the meaning of the song – if it has one. What might take us there is "Sad-Eyed Lady's" place on "Blonde on Blonde", and how it completes and refers back to many of the themes on that album, and more widely to a central

---

11   Marshall, L. (2009) "Bob Dylan and the Academy". In Kevin Dettmar (ed) *The Cambridge Companion to Bob Dylan*. Cambridge: Cambridge University Press, pp. 100
12   Bangs, L. (2004) "Love of Confusion." In B. Hedin (ed) *The Bob Dylan Reader. Studio A*. New York: Norton, p. 156.

common poetic denominator of modern western literature. "Blonde on Blonde" is an album about, among other things, waiting, jealous love, sexual longing, and the threat of women's sexuality, and "Sad-Eyed Lady" has something to say about all of these. The song also follows a particular tradition of love poems, which helps us understand it in the context of the many writers who have dwelt on similar themes. So when we hear "Sad-Eyed Lady", we don't just hear this song, we hear as well echoed in the song the many women on "Blonde on Blonde" and in literary history.

Let's start with "Sad-Eyed Lady's" obscure chorus:

> *Sad-eyed lady of the lowlands,*
> *Where the sad-eyed prophet says that no man comes,*
> *My warehouse eyes, my Arabian drums,*
> *Should I leave them by your gate,*
> *Or, sad-eyed lady, should I wait?*

That final evocative couplet begins to pull the album together by taking us back to earlier songs on the album and echoing other gates and waiting. In "I Want You", the rhyme is internal and it's someone else doing the waiting:

> *The drunken politician leaps*
> *Upon the street where mothers weep*
> *And the saviors who are fast asleep,*
> *They wait for you.*
> *And I wait for them to interrupt*

> *Me drinkin' from my broken cup*
> *And ask me to*
> *Open up the gate for you.*

In a third song, "Absolutely Sweet Marie", the rhyme is more deeply hidden, and both the singer and everybody else are waiting:

> *Well, your railroad gate, you know I just can't jump it*
> *Sometimes it gets so hard, you see….*

> *Well, I waited for you when I was half sick*
> *Yes, I waited for you when you hated me*
> *Well, I waited for you inside of the frozen traffic*

> *Well, I don't know how it happened*
> *But the river-boat captain, he knows my fate*
> *But ev'rybody else, even yourself*
> *They're just gonna have to wait.* [13]

So when we get to the "gate/wait" rhyme on "Sad-Eyed Lady" it sends us back to these two other songs. Dylan is still waiting at the gate thirty or so years later when he returned to this rhyme in "Can't Wait" from "Time out of Mind", released in 1997, still trying to figure out if he should be waiting or not:

> *I'm breathing hard, standing at the gate*

---

[13]   Waiting is peculiar to "Blonde on Blonde" as we'll see in the last chapter of this book.

But I don't know how much longer I can wait.[14]

Or perhaps when he came to the end of "Sad-Eyed Lady" Dylan had other meanings of the word "wait" in mind. As an intransitive verb wait means to be waiting for someone, the most obvious meaning here, but also to attend with ceremony and respect (to wait on you). As a transitive verb, wait means to serenade in the early morning or late at night, and "Sad-Eyed Lady" certainly has something of the serenade about it.

On "Blonde on Blonde" the gate image is a barrier, to the sad-eyed lady, to Sweet Marie, and to the wanted woman – and in all cases perhaps a barrier to sex. When Dylan wrote about gates, he had exclusion on his mind, not only in these songs, but also on "Temporary Like Achilles":

Just what do you think you have to guard?

How come you send someone out to have me barred?

Achilles is in your alleyway,
He don't want me here,
He does brag.

---

14   Gray (p. 828) points to the Guthrie song "Waiting at the Gate" as a potential source for this rhyme. Dylan may have been thinking about "Blonde on Blonde" when he wrote "Time out of Mind". Several commentators have pointed out that "Highlands" refers back to "Sad Eyed Lady of the Lowlands", and "Highlands" includes the line: "Wouldn't know the difference between a real blonde and a fake".

He's pointing to the sky
And he's hungry, like a man in drag.[15]
How come you get someone like him to be your
guard?
You know I want your lovin',
Honey, but you're so hard.

So it shouldn't come as a surprise that there's some-one saying "no man comes" at the end of the last track of "Blonde on Blonde". And as we'll see in Chapter 4, gates and barred entries are themes that have fascinated Dylan throughout his career.

There's another theme on "Blonde on Blonde" that "Sad-Eyed Lady" neatly rounds off, when the sad-eyed prophet says that no man comes. Because there are a lot of "third people", like temporary Achilles, on "Blonde on Blonde", getting in the way – in fact on almost every song, in a number of varia-tions. We've already seen the saviours who are fast

---

15   Why a man in drag? Is it just a handy rhyme with "brag". According to Ovid's "Metamorphoses". Achilles did get dressed up in drag one time. "Knowing her son was destined to die if he went to fight in the Trojan war, Thethis, a sea nymph, disguised Achilles as a woman and entrusted him to King Lycomedes, in whose palace on the isle of Scyros he lived among the king's daughters. Odysseus and other Greek chieftains were sent to fetch Achilles. They cunningly laid a heap of gifts before the girls - jewellery, clothes and other finery, but among them a sword, spear and shield. When a trumpet was sounded, Achilles instinctively snatched up the weapons and thus betrayed his identity." See the painting "The Discovery of Achilles among the Daughters of Lycomedes"
http://www.wga.hu/frames-e.html?/html/b/bray/jan/lycomede.html
But why a man in drag should be hungry, I have no idea. We come back to the same theme with five believers dressed like men on "Obviously Five Believers".

asleep waiting for the gate to be opened in "I Want You", and the Persian drunkard following to absolutely sweet Marie's house, but there are several others.

We start off with "Pledging My Time":

Well, the hobo jumped up,
He came down natur'lly.
After he stole my baby,
Then he wanted to steal me.

"He stole my baby" – where have we heard this before? Just about every romantic singer and poet has written about love lost to another– to a man or woman, or to death, as in Blake's fragment "Never Seek to Tell Thy Love":

Soon as she was gone from me
A traveller came by
Silently, invisibly–
He took her with a sigh.

The next intruder on "Blonde on Blonde" is the little boy lost in "Visions of Johanna":

Little boy lost he takes himself so seriously
He brags of his misery
He likes to live dangerously
And when bringing her name up
He speaks of a farewell kiss to me

Then there's someone being taken for a ride on "I Want You":

Now your dancing child with his Chinese suit,
He spoke to me, I took his flute.
No, I wasn't very cute to him,
Was I?
But I did it, though, because he lied
Because he took you for a ride
And because time was on his side...

Drunken Persian, little boy, dancing child – surely an attempt at a put down of a rival.

The same theme continues on "One of Us Must Know (Sooner or Later)", where a friend appears:

When I heard you say goodbye to your friend and smile
I thought it was well understood
That you'd be coming back in a little while
I didn't know you'd be saying goodbye for good

And then there's the doctor and the new boy friend in "Leopard-Skin Pill-Box Hat":

I asked the doctor if I could see you
It's bad for your health he said
Yes I disobeyed his orders
I came to see you
But I found him there instead   ·
I don't mind him cheating on me....

Well see you got a new boy friend
Well I never seen him before

I saw you making love with him
You forgot to close the garage door....

Dylan's not done there, there's the judge, and the other kind of lover whose has a different kissing technique in "Most Likely You Go Your Way (And I'll Go Mine)": But, later on "One of Us Must Know (Sooner or Later)" the tables are turned, and we come across a reversed theme, the singer caught between two women:

When you whispered in my ear
And asked me if I was leaving with you or her
I didn't realize just what I did hear
I didn't realize how young you were[16]

There's also the debutante and Ruthie vying for his attention knowing what he wants and needs on "Stuck Inside of Mobile with the Memphis Blues Again":

When Ruthie says come see her
In her honky tonk lagoon
Where I can watch her waltz for free
Neath the Panamanian moon
And I say "come on now
You know about my debutante"
And she says "Your debutante just knows what you need
But I know what you want"

---

16   Or as Dylan sings it:

How yoooooooouuuuunnnnnggggg you weeerrrrrrrrrrrrrrrrrrrrrrrrrrrrrrrrrrrrrrrrr reeeeeeeeeeeeeeeeeeerrrrrrrrrrrrrrrr

And there's a threesome again in "4ᵗʰ Time Around":

*She screamed till her face got so red then she fell
on the floor
And I covered her up and thought I'd go look
through her drawer*

*And when I was through I filled up my shoe and
brought it to you*

It was a while before Dylan came back, poignantly, to this theme, on "You're a Big Girl Now" from "Blood on the Tracks", released in 1975:

*Love is so simple, to quote a phrase,
You've known it all the time, I'm learnin' it these
days.
Oh, I know where I can find you, oh, oh,
In somebody's room.
It's a price I have to pay
You're a big girl all the way.*

Jealous love and infidelity are among western society's most passionate interests, stretching from Chaucer to Jane Austen to Woody Allen and Bertolucci (see their movies "The Dreamers" and "Vicky Christina Barcelona"). It's an instantly recognizable literary theme that Dylan reworks in the smoky claustrophobic atmosphere of "Blonde on Blonde". So when we get to the end of "Sad-Eyed Lady" we've already been through at least ten references to infidelity and that suspicious sad-eyed prophet who pops up in the chorus is just the last of these rivalrous and challenging figures.

What else is there to say about the chorus of "Sad-Eyed Lady" which tells us that, rather than having bought one and a half albums, we have instead a song that ties up the other themes on "Blonde on Blonde"?

With your sad-eyed prophet says that no man comes. [17]

It's that word "comes" which is everywhere on "Blonde on Blonde". It's on "4th Time Around", the song that precedes "Sad Eyed Lady" on the album except for one, and the most blatantly sexual song on the album, which also repeats the "drum/come" rhyme:[18]

---

17   Ricks (104-5) traces these lines to the Bible: "Where the sad-eyed prophet says that no man comes": the phrase "no man" comes more than once in the book of Ezekiel, and there is a gate nearby. Ezekiel 44:2: "This gate shall be shut, it shall not be opened, and no man shall enter by it." (Similarly, 14: 15: "that no man may pass through".) "No man is heard again and again in the Bible. Isaiah 24: 10: "Every house is shut up, that no man may come in. There is a crying for wine in the streets; all joy is darkened, the mirth of the land is gone. In the city is left desolation, and the gate is smitten with destruction."

18   Dylan may have picked up the repetition from some blues songs dealing with infidelity, for example, Charles Davenport's, "I Ain't No Ice Man" from 1938. Or Papa Charlie Jackson's "Hot Papa Blues" recorded in 1925:

I ain't no coalman: ain't no coalman's son
But I can keep you warm: until your coalman comes
Won't you tell me pretty mama: I won't have to wait
Will I be your regular: or did I come too late
I may look green: but I ain't no clown

I stood there and hummed,
I tapped on her drum and asked her how come.
And she buttoned her boot,
And straightened her suit,
Then she said, "Don't get cute."
So I forced my hands in my pockets
And felt with my thumbs,
And gallantly handed her
My very last piece of gum.

Her Jamaican rum
And when she did come, I asked her for some.

This approaches the intentionally crude sexual innuendo of the Basement Tapes:

Well, I'm hittin' it too hard
My stones won't take
I get up in the mornin'
But it's too early to wake

Bo Chatman's "All Around Man" recorded in 1936, leaves little to the imagination. Bo Chatman played with the Mississippi Sheikhs, who we know Dylan admires because he included two of their songs on "World Gone Wrong" and refers to them in "Chronicles":

Now I ain't no butcher: no butcher's son
I can do your cutting: until the butcher man comes
Now I ain't no plumber: no plumber's son
I can do your screwing: till the plumber man comes
Now I ain't no miller: no miller's son
I can do your grinding: till the miller-man comes
Dylan used the same idiom on the unreleased "Long Time Gone",
recorded in 1962:
But I know I ain't no prophet
An' I ain't no prophet's son.

First it's hello, goodbye
Then push and then crash

Ev'rybody from right now
To over there and back
The louder they come
The harder they crack
Come now, sweet cream
Don't forget to flash
We're all gonna meet
At that million dollar bash

Similarly on "Pledging my Time" from "Blonde on Blonde":

Won't you come with me, baby?
I'll take you where you wanna go.

But I'm pledging my time to you,
Hopin' you'll come through, too.

And "Temporary like Achilles":

How come you send someone out to have me barred?
You know I want your lovin',
Honey, why are you so hard?

How come you get someone like him to be your guard?

How many times does Dylan need to sing the word "come" before we get it? As Gray commented,

"Blonde on Blonde" is an album saturated with the blues, and the blues is a genre saturated with sex. Feeling in his pockets with his thumbs, the fever down in his pockets, the chambermaid who knows where he wants to be, making love to the women who's just like a woman, Louise and her lover so entwined, making love in the garage wearing a leopard-skin pill box hat, the lonesome organ grinder crying (anything to do with grinding in the blues relates to sex, so an organ grinder isn't just playing a musical instrument[19]), the washed out horns ("horn" being slang for an erection), "I want you/I want you/I want you so bad", "too long they've been without it/Because I don't think about it", she knows where he'd like to be, and so on, it's an album full of wants and needs.

So by the time we get to the chorus of "Sad-Eyed Lady of the Lowlands" the drum/come rhyme echoes what we've heard a number of times:

> Sad-eyed lady of the lowlands
> With your sad-eyed prophet says that no man comes

Strange that no man comes, because aren't the Kings of Tyrus waiting in line for their geranium kiss, and who among them just wants to kiss her? And isn't the singer trying to figure out if he should wait?

---

19   As in Victoria Spivey's "Organ Grinder Blues", recorded in 1928, the same Victoria Spivey shown on the back cover of "New Morning" – the photo being from 1962 although "New Morning" was released in 1970.

Goddess or whore?

Is there an intimation of prostitution here in all of the references to women behind locked doors and gates? Is "Sad-Eyed Lady" ambivalent about woman as whore, and woman as mother/goddess? As Charles Shaar Murray wrote in 1989: "Sixties songwriters refused women any middle ground between the pedestal and the gutter."[20] Not only sixties songwriters of course, because there's a lot of poems and songs about women as prostitutes/goddesses. The threat of women's sexuality goes back to Eve in the Garden of Eden and before, and has governed institutionalised religion in different cultures down the ages, which have portrayed women's sexuality as a fatal attraction. The young woman who wins the narrator's heart in Umberto Eco's "Name of the Rose" is a perfect symbol of society's ambivalence about women – the first love who is never forgotten, and almost immolated as a witch. There is also the blues tradition about prostitution in songs Dylan knew well and recorded, for example "Frankie and Johnnie" from the early 1900s, "The House of the Rising Sun" (from 1937), and "Blood in My Eyes", a Mississippi Sheiks song Dylan recorded on "World Gone Wrong" in 1993. The common poetic denominator here is the tension between the attractions and threats of women, as seen by men writing about them.

---

20   Quoted in Greil Marcus (2005) *Like a Rolling Stone. Bob Dylan at the Crossroads. An explosion of vision and humor that forever changed pop music*. New York: Public Affairs.

The thin dividing line between love and fear perhaps accounts for so many critics discomfort with "Sad-Eyed Lady". In her *Encyclopaedia of Prostitution and Sex Work*, Melissa Ditmore writes about representations of one of the best known reformed prostitutes turned goddess, Mary Magdalene:

> *The most positive depiction of a prostitute in medieval writing, however, was the character of Mary Magdalene inherited from the New Testament…..Medieval writers expanded on…accounts of Mary Magdalene in a variety of ways. First, medieval tradition believed Mary Magdalene to have been a prostitute. …..Finally, the Magdalene becomes a central figure in medieval hagiographies. Probably the best-known example is the hagiography written by the Dominican monk, Jacobus de Voragine (cs. 1230-98 C.E.)…. Here, the reformed prostitute is swept across the sea to Marseilles, where she converts the pagan Romans to Christianity, despite the local governor's interference. She performs a miracle by resurrecting a woman, and she lives as a hermit for 30 years before her death. After her death, her body become incorruptible.*[21]

Ah, our fascination with women's bodies, even after their deaths!!! One of the original sad-eyed ladies is another Madonna, mother Mary, who wept at her

---

21   Ditmore, M. (2006) *Encyclopedia of Prostitution and Sex Work*. Greenwood Press, 295.

son's death. Marina Warner's book on the cult of the Virgin Mary is a learned discussion of the representations of Mary through history, and for example recounts Jacopone's hymn of the passion Donna del Paradiso, where Christ calls to Mary: "Mamma, why have you come? You cause me a mortal wound, for your weeping pierces me and seems to me the sharpest sword."[22] But sad-eyed and weeping women predate this according to Warner, for example to the Goddess Isis holding the body of her son.

Ricks draws a neat parallel between "Sad-Eyed Lady" and Swinburne's "Dolores", which Ricks calls Swinburne's anti-prayer to his anti-madonna. "Dolores" starts:

> Cold eyelids that hide like a jewel
> Hard eyes that grow soft for an hour;
> The heavy white limbs, and the cruel
> Red mouth like a venomous flower;
> When these are gone by with their glories,
> What shall rest of thee then, what remain,
> O mystic and sombre Dolores,
> Our Lady of Pain?

Ricks also quotes Keats' "La Belle Dame Sans Merci" as one of many mythical poems and stories which tell of the danger and attractiveness of women without mercy.

---

22   Warner, M. (1990) *Alone of All Her Sex. The Myth and Cult of the Virgin Mary*. London: Picador.

There are other references to prostitution in Dylan's songs, for example in "Chimes of Freedom", released in 1964:

Tolling for the deaf an' blind, tolling for the mute
Tolling for the mistreated, mateless mother, the mistitled prostitute
For the misdemeanor outlaw, chased an' cheated by pursuit

And on "Jokerman" Dylan wrote in 1983 or thereabouts:

It's a shadowy world, skies are slippery gray,
A woman just gave birth to a prince today and dressed him in scarlet.
He'll put the priest in his pocket, put the blade to the heat,
Take the motherless children off the street
And place them at the feet of a harlot.[23]

What's interesting in these quotes is the proximity of "mother" and "prostitute/harlot" – as Blake put it in "To the Accuser Who is the God of This World": "Every Harlot was a Virgin Once", and here is Blake hearing curses blasting infants in "London":

---

23   In "Simple Twist of Fate", released on "Blood on the Tracks" in 1975, the encounter as Dylan originally conceptualised it looks like it was with a prostitute – there's more on this later in this chapter.

But most, through midnight streets I hear
How the youthful harlot's curse
Blasts the new-born infant's tear,
And blights with plagues the marriage-hearse.

The ladies treat me kindly

While "Blonde on Blonde" ends with one sad-eyed lady, there are plenty of other references to suspicious women and ladies on the album. Groups of powerful ladies on the outskirts of society are a literary archetype, for example the Amazons and the Valkyries, or, another modern day version, the witches in Philip Pulman's "The Golden Compass".[24] The "they" (they'll stone you when you do this or that) on the raucous "Rainy Day Women #12 and 35", the first track of "Blonde on Blonde" are the first group of ladies we encounter, although Dylan doesn't mix sex and drugs on this song.

Whatever "Visions of Johanna" is about, the smoky, crowded rooms and eccentric imagery are a backdrop for the goings on of the night, with the ladies playing blindman's bluff, and the all-night girls whispering, and where there is a hidden lady:

In the empty lot where the ladies play blindman's
bluff with the key chain
And the all-night girls they whisper of escapades
out on the "D" train

---

24   See P. Brunel (1992)(ed.) *Companion to Literary Myths, Heroes and Archetypes*. London: Routledge.

We can hear the night watchman click his flashlight
Ask himself if it's him or them that's really insane.[25]

The *click* of the flash light takes us right back to the *tricks* in the first line in this hyper-alliterative song (which reminds us in turn of the lights *flick*ering in the opposite loft – trick, click and flick playing with night and light), which sets its tone:

Ain't it just like the night to play tricks when you're trying to be so quiet

"Ain't it just the night to play tricks"? Well is it or ain't it? Is that, like, a rhetorical question? Don't we already all know that it's just like the night to play tricks when we're trying to be so quiet? Or is this Dylan just playing tricks with this kick-assonanced line, full of "t"s, "s"s and "k"s, so by the time we get to the end of the second line we do feel kind of stranded:

We sit here stranded, though we're all doin' our best to deny it

Thirteen "t"s. four "st"s and one almost "st" (sit), a half rhyme on "night" and "quiet" and "deny it", a quarter rhyme on "like" and night", even a rhyme on "ain't it" and "sit", all in two lines – not bad![26]

---

25   That last line has given Dylan problems in concert, not surprising as it's 23 syllables.

26   Dylan used the same rhyme on "Farewell Angelina", written around the same time but unreleased until the *Bootleg Series 1-3* in 1991:

But, back to the question, "ain't it just like night to play tricks"? It is, because the night playing tricks, in the context of those all night girls whispering of escapades, and the other sexual references on the album, refers to the slang meaning of the term, which is the sexual act between a prostitute and customer.[27] And what I like about the beginning of this song is the way the question draws us right in – we have to figure out if it's just like the night to play tricks when we're trying to be so quiet.

Dylan doesn't often personify the night – perhaps "Visions of Johanna" is the only time – but it is a favourite image, as in the night blowing cold and rainy in "Love Minus Zero/No Limit", and the silent night shattering in "One Too Many Mornings". Dylan is not alone in imagining the night as a prostitute, e.e. cummings went there in "Paris", published in 1928":

this April sunset completely utters
utters serenely silently a cathedral
before whose upward lean magnificent face
the streets turn young with rain...

Call me any name you like
I will never deny it
Farewell Angelina
The sky is erupting
I must go where it's quiet.

The sense here is quite different from "Visions of Johanna" as this rhyme brings closure to the song, in the same way that Hamlet's last line "The rest is silence" closes on the end of noise.

27   See the use of the term "tricks of a whore" from "Annachie Gordon" later in this chapter.

while
there and here the lithe indolent prostitute
Night, argues
with certain houses

To get back to the ladies, a term that Dylan is anachronistically fond of, who are those ladies on "Stuck Inside of Mobile"?

The ladies treat me kindly
And furnish me with tape
But deep inside my heart
I know I can't escape

There are plenty of other ladies on "Blonde on Blonde" than these and the Sad-Eyed Lady - the Queen of Spades (perhaps from Robert Johnson's "Queen of Spades"[28]), the French girl, mothers weeping, the debutante, the countess, Madonna, Mona Lisa, Mona, Ruthie, and Sweet Marie among others. Given the constant references to infidelity and sexual desire, we have to assume that there is something suspect about the sad-eyed lady who ends the album, whose flesh is like silk, and whose attributes are listed one by one.

Blason

Perhaps "Sad-Eyed Lady of the Lowlands" isn't drivel after all!!! And, as it turns out, the song fits sweetly into

---

28   Johnson recorded "Little Queen of Spades" in 1937.

a long tradition of "love" poems known as "blason", which Belknap defines as[29]:

> *a poetic genre dedicated to the praise of the female by the particularization of her attributes. This technique conventionally allowed the poet to describe or metaphorically elaborate one feature per line, creating a vertical compilation whose constituents are thematically continuous but linearly independent.*

Basically, a poem about different parts of the female body. Belknap gives an example of traditional blason from Bartholomew Griffin, the 16th century English poet:

> *My Lady's hair is threads of beaten gold,*
> *Her front the purest Chrystal eye hath seen:*
> *Her eyes the brightest stars the heavens hold,*
> *Her cheeks red roses such as seld have been….*

Belknap writes:[30]

> *As convention the blason typically presented the mistress's features in a fixed sequence, and as a convention it typically invited talented writers to challenge its principles, to dazzle, and to create lasting art…In its listing of attributes, the blason provides a sequence that is voyeuristically*

29   Belknap, R. (2004) *The List. The Uses and Pleasures of Cataloguing*. New Haven: Yale University Press,
30   pp. 24-5.

followed by the reader. Poets arranged the individual features to guide the reader through a particular way of seeing the beloved. By convention, it usually followed a head-to-toe sequence, but often it is not so much the contents of the sequence but the arrangement and manipulation (where does it start, where does it end) that reveal its underlying purpose. In a head-to-toe description, it is nearly impossible to develop an emotional climax peeking at the beloved's feet. Recognizing this, poets have manipulated the form by arranging its components for more satisfactory results. Some poems may linger on specific elements, shifting the emphasis or abandoning the convention. Some may abbreviate the enumeration by leaving off at strategically suggestive locations. Still others may use the sequence of comparisons to progress not in a direction of physical observation but into a different dimension altogether: away from corporeal loveliness toward a transcending spiritual beauty.

Shakespeare's Sonnet 130 is a favourite example:

My mistress' eyes are nothing like the sun;
Coral is far more red than her lips' red;
If snow be white, why then her breasts are dun;
If hairs be wires, black wires grow on her head.
I have seen roses damask'd, red and white,
But no such roses see I in her cheeks;
And in some perfumes is there more delight
Than in the breath that from my mistress reeks.

> *I love to hear her speak, yet well I know*
> *That music hath a far more pleasing sound;*
> *I grant I never saw a goddess go;*
> *My mistress, when she walks, treads on the*
> *ground:*
> *And yet, by heaven, I think my love as rare*
> *As any she belied with false compare.*

Was Dylan aware of this tradition? Who knows, but "Sad-Eyed Lady" follows the traditional blason progression, starting like Shakespeare's Sonnet 130 with the eyes and mouth:

> *With your mercury mouth in the missionary times*
> *And your eyes like smoke and your prayers like*
> *rhymes*

Proceeding downwards, to the well protected pockets and the belt like lace, to the feet:

> *They wished you'd accepted the blame for the*
> *farm,*
> *But with the sea at your feet and the phony false*
> *alarm*

And, at the final end, returning to that "hollow" face and progressing to a transcending beauty, but an empty spirituality:

> *And your saintlike face and your ghostlike soul*

So Ricks is right to draw the comparison between "Sad- Eyed Lady" and Swinburne's "Dolores",

because both list the venomously attractive prop-
erties of women one by one as part of the blason
tradition. When we hear "Sad-Eyed Lady" we hear
as well echoes of the ambivalence of men writing
through the ages about the temptations of women.
"I Shall Be Free", released three years before "Sad-
Eyed Lady", is an early attempt at a blason:

> *Well, I took me a woman late last night,*
> *I's three-fourths drunk, she looked uptight.*
> *She took off her wheel, took off her bell,*
> *Took off her wig, said, "How do I smell?"*
> *I hot-footed it . . . bare-naked . . .*
> *Out the window!*[31]

"Sad-Eyed Lady" is closer to an anti-blason, with a
high level of ambivalence concerning the object
of attention. Dylan summarizes this ambivalence in
exquisitely ambiguous writing:

> *And your magazine husband who one day just*
> *had to go*

Did he have to go in the sense of "I just had to get
rid of him" or "those old chairs had to go because

---

31   On "The Freewheelin' Bob Dylan" Dylan sings:

Well, I took me a woman late last night,
I's three-fourths drunk, she looked allright.
Till she started peeling off her onion gook
Took off her wig, said, "How do I look?"
I hot-footed it . . . bare-naked . . .
Out the window

I couldn't stand them any longer"? Or did he just have to go because he could no longer stand being with her? The phrase "just had to go" ("just" being another of those words that is repeated many times on "Blonde and Blonde", including twice on "Visions of Johanna", and of course on "Just Like a Woman") means we will never know. Similarly the next line:

And your gentleness now, which you just can't help but show

That same ambivalence hinging on the word "just"; she just can't help showing her gentleness, making this a back-handed compliment at best.

"Sad-Eyed Lady" reads like a list of attributes, and because it's a list, nouns are predominant. This means an absence of verbs, and that the sad-eyed lady hardly does anything – ok, she places her street car visions on the grass, can't help but show her gentleness, and her fingertips fold around the holy medallion, but that's about it. As Krein and Levin have noted, agency is not high on the list of the women in Dylan's songs, rather they are the singer's objects.[32]

The use of nouns is interesting. Because in the same way that Dylan has used adverbs as adjectives in the titles of some of the songs on "Blonde on Blonde" ("Temporary Like Achilles", "Absolutely

32   Krein, K. and A. Levin (2006) "Just Like a Woman: Dylan, Authenticity, and the Second Sex." In P. Vernezzee and C. Porter Bob Dylan and Philosophy Chicago: Open Court, 53-65.

Sweet Marie", "Obviously Five Believers"), in "Sad-Eyed Lady" he uses nouns as adjectives in a way that challenges the listener to figure out if this combination makes any sense. Are we in the midst of a stream of consciousness, where words are interchangeable as long as they sound good, about which I write more in the next chapter?

With your mercury mouth in the missionary times

You could have "sweet mouth", "hard mouth" or "silver mouth", you could have good times or bad times, but in English you can't have a mercury mouth and missionary times. "Blonde on Blonde" is an apt title for an album where so many nouns are joined together.

Not only that, but the nouns he uses just don't fit together in any way that makes sense other than through word association. The words are so vague that they could have multiple – or no – meanings. And that's the beauty of the song, we are left to figure for ourselves what these word associations mean. Belknap writes on the use of nouns in poetic lists[33]:

> *The list is a device that writers have frequently employed to display the pleasurable infinitude of language.*
>
> *The stacked lines of a verse provide virtual ledger entries in which the poet can itemize,*

---

33   Pp. 2, 15, 19-20.

registering and elaborating a certain number of items per line…. This loose framework lets the poet enumerate or accumulate, amplify or distribute, mount or diminish, suggest completion or unending plenitude, according to a custom-made formula.

This is to say that usually nouns are compiled, whether persons, found objects, store inventories, features of an individual, or the days of the year. This is particularly true of non-literary compilations – for example, where a record is kept of units of currency or particular events. But in the literary sphere to list nouns is to more than record; it is to display, to lay out, to arrange – to create reality – whether that be to represent a moment of complete awareness of the world or just to experiment, to conjure by naming.

But let's go back to where we started this chapter, does "Sad-Eyed Lady" have any meaning? As Scobie has suggested[34]:

Much of Dylan's poetry in the mid-1960s was indebted to this reading of the French Symbolist poets, especially Rimbaud, who were also influential in the development of French Surrealist painting in the 1920s. A central technique of Surrealism, the sudden juxtaposition of bizarrely unrelated objects, was derived from a line by Lautreamont:

---

34   p.268.

"the chance meeting, on a dissection table, of an umbrella and sewing-machine."

So are those opening lines the sudden juxtaposition of bizarrely unrelated object?

With your mercury mouth in the missionary times,
And your eyes like smoke and your prayers like rhymes,
And your silver cross, and your voice like chimes,
Oh, who among them do they think could bury you?

Maybe, but there is a lot to make of these lines, some of it due perhaps to the serendipity of the English language, some due perhaps to the hyperactive nature of Dylan's creative process. The first noun Dylan chose, "mercury", has a number of connotations. There is mercury the metal, and the metal that is used in people's mouth for dental repair. There is mercury the medicine, which used to be used as cure for sexually transmitted diseases. There is mercury which is quicksilver, which chimes nicely with the silver cross in the third line of the song. And mercury is also Mercury the winged messenger, Hermes, so why not have a "mercury mouth" if you are going to be the god of communication, because, after all, we communicate through our mouths a lot of the time. Similarly with "missionary times"; is there a reference to the "missionary position" which is the only time that "missionary" is used as an adjective? And do the "missionary times" refer forwards to the "magazine husband" later in the song, the times being among other things a newspaper? Perhaps the point of these lines and parts of this song are that they are purposely open to multiple interpretations.

The ambivalence about the "Sad-Eyed Lady" comes across in the song's second and third lines:

> And your eyes like smoke[35] and your prayers like rhymes,
> And your silver cross, and your voice like chimes

First there is the religious association which occurs throughout the song – the prayers, the silver cross, the holy medallion, her gypsy hymns, the dead angels, her saint-like face, her ghost-like soul, the sad-eyed prophet – all of which remind us of the madonna and the mother goddess side of the madonna/whore equation. But.... "prayers like rhymes"? Is this also a backhanded compliment? Prayers are meant to be incantations that link the prayer with a deity, so should they be like rhymes, which are children's' prayers perhaps, and note here "rhyme" is a noun, not a verb. Dylan could have written "prayers that rhyme" but that would have taken away from the repetition of "like".

---

35   No smoke without fire, so the smoking eyes are followed later in the song by "midnight flames". And this is a song with a focus on eyes, as in the following:

Eyes like smoke
Street car visions
My warehouse eyes
Into your eyes where the moonlight swims

At the end of the song Dylan slips in a marvellous inversion, and concision of the first order, again challenging us to come to terms with the rubble of language which makes up the song. The last line of the song is:

And your saint like face and your ghost like soul

We've heard so many "likes" on this album that there's little surprise that Dylan ends with two similes that sum up the "Sad-Eyed Lady" – external beauty, but nothing on the inside – or is this what the line means? The first simile – a face like a saint's – is commonplace. Van Morrison uses a similar simile at the end of "Sweet Thing". Of course, if this woman is part madonna, she needs to have a face like a saint. Dylan uses the word "saint' sparingly in his songs, although he's fond of religious imagery. "If you see Saint Annie" he sings in "Just Like Tom Thumb Blues" written around the same time as "Sad-Eyed Lady", a song which also refers to a ghost, but in this case looking just like one:

And picking up Angel who
Just arrived here from the coast
Who looked so fine at first
But left looking just like a ghost

Then there's the echo back to that favorite line of everyone's in the companion song to "Sad-Eyed Lady" on "Blonde on Blonde", "Visions of Johanna", but in the latter it's the women's face that is ghostlike:

Ghosts of electricity howl in the bones of her face.

But "ghost like soul" from "Sad-Eyed Lady" is something else, completely. If "your saint like face" is an abbreviation for "and your face like a saint's face", then "ghost like soul" should be short for "your soul like a ghost's soul". So what's a ghost's soul like? Do ghosts have souls – or, aren't they meant to be the souls of the departed?

So, I at least, got my money's worth when I bought the **four** sided album "Blonde on Blonde".

Love and money

The tension between love and money is played out in thousands of songs, novels, poems and movies. As 17th century English poet Samuel Butler put it in his ironic poem "Hudibras": "For money has a power above/ The stars, and fate, to manage love." It is one of the most consistent themes in western literature, with a distinct preference among writers for true love over false money. Avarice – excessive or insatiable desire for gain or wealth – gets a bad rap through history. Of course the writers criticizing those desiring money often have sufficient quantities themselves, but that's another story.[36] It links as well to the goddess/whore contrast just discussed. The contrast between heavenly love and earthly pursuits structures much western

---

36   On which see Delany, P. (2002) *Literature, Money and the Market: From Trollope to Amis*. New York: Palgrave

medieval literature, including Chaucer's "Canterbury Tales" and the Arthurian myths. It is the central motif in "Pride and Prejudice", where, in early nineteenth century Britain (as is many parts of the developing world today, and retained in western wedding ceremonies where the father symbolically "gives away" his daughter to her soon to be husband, with the bride standing on the left to denote her inferior position) women are property to be handed from father to husband, rather than marrying for love; but Jane Austen breaks the rules and ends up with both love and money, demonstrating, perhaps, that they are not incompatible – we don't always have to be rich and loveless, or poor and loved.

In his study of literature, money and the market, Paul Delany comments on the "market for women"[37]:

> *Richardson inaugurates, and Trollope concludes, the high era of the "marriage novel" that takes as its matter the interaction between love, family and economic interest, within the constraints set by the marriage system of upper-class English society. Richardson shows the system leading to tragedy; Thackeray sees in it "the grim workings of marital capitalism"; Austen and Trollope are much more inclined to grant, for their heroes and heroines at least, a happier balance between self-expression and the observance of social and economic norms….The aristocratic*

---

37   Delany, P. (2002) *Literature, Money and the Market: From Trollope to Amis*. New York: Palgrave, pp 32-3.

> marriage system rests on the contradiction that a woman is a person, with whom one can fall in love, but she is also an exchangeable asset, priced by her degree of wealth, beauty, and gentility. ...As Byron put it: "Money is the magnet; as to Women, one is as well as another."

Women being forced to forsake a loved one at the command of their father, or men choosing money over love, are common motifs in many folk ballads, for example "Auchanachie Gordon", one of the Child Ballads - covered by Lorrena McKennit among many others – here's one verse:

> Auchanachie Gordon is bonny and braw,
> He would tempt any woman that ever he saw;
> He would tempt any woman, so has he tempted me,
> And I'll die if i getna my love Auchanachie.'
> In came her father, tripping on the floor,
> Says, Jeanie, ye're trying the tricks o a whore;
> Ye're caring for them that cares little for thee;
> Ye must marry Salton, leave Auchanachie.
> 'Auchanachie Gordon, he is but a man;
> Altho he be pretty, where lies his free land?
> Salton's lands they lie broad, his towers they stand hie,
> Ye must marry Salton, leave Auchanachie

As I noted, there's a clever twist here as Jeannie's father calls her a whore, whereas she is motivated by love and her father by money.

"As I Roved Out", another traditional folk ballad, deals with the same theme:

As I roved out one bright May morning
To view the purple heather and flowers gay
Who should I spy but my own true lover
As she sat under yon willow tree
I took off my hat and I did salute her
I did salute her most courageously
When she turned around
And the tears fell from her eyes
Saying 'False young man, you have deluded me

Three diamond rings for love I gave you
Three diamond rings to wear on your right hand
But the vows you made, love
You went and broke them
And married the lassie that had the land.'

'If I married the lassie that had the land, my love
'Tis that I'll rue until the day I die
But when fortune calls few men can shun it
I was a blind fool was I'

Now at night when I go to my bed of slumber
The thoughts of my true love run in my mind
When I turned around to embrace my darling
Instead of gold 'tis brass I find

The ballad "The Gypsy Laddie", from which Dylan drew for "Boots of Spanish Leather", and which he recorded as "Black Jack Davy" in 1992 on "Good

As I Been To You", is another example, as is the "The Butcher Boy":

> There is an inn in that same town,
> And there my love he sits him down;
> He takes a strange girl on his knee
> And tells her what he wouldn't tell me.
>
> The reason is, I'll tell you why,
> Because she's got more gold than I.
> But gold will melt and silver fly,
> And in time of need be as poor as I.

The tensions between love and money are mainstreamed into the English language. Blake's fragment "Never seek to tell thy love", which I use throughout this book, encapsulates this tension in a line that revolves around the dual meaning of "tell":

> Never seek to tell thy love,
> Love that never told can be;
> For the gentle wind does move,
> Silently, invisibly.
>
> I told my love, I told my love,
> I told her all my heart;
> Trembling, cold, in ghastly fears,
> Ah! she doth depart.

For Blake, "tell" means to speak and to count. Thus the origins of the phrase "teller", as in "bank teller" – someone who counts money. So the first line of the fragment means both "don't tell your love that you love her", and "don't try to count your love like you would count money." Because counting your love like money means that she will certainly depart (maybe even in ghastly fears). "Account" has a similar dual meaning in English, to count something or to given an account in the sense of recounting.

The English language is peculiarly mercantile in its terms of endearment. Words that are used every day by millions of loved ones reveal this – precious (used by Gollum in "Lord of the Rings" to describe the gold ring that eventually destroys him); dear (which used to start every letter, and still starts millions of emails every day - chere has the same dual meaning in French); value, as in "I really value our relationship"; prized, treasured, and so on. The term "interest" as in "to be interested in someone" also has another meaning of "to pay interest".

The contrast between love and money takes writers to one of the most deep-seated of human dilemmas – should we choose material possessions before passion, and is it really possible to have both? No surprise given its predominance in western literature as well as folk and blues songs, that Dylan uses the tension between love and money to structure some of his love songs. One of my favorite Dylan songs, "Spanish Boots of Spanish Leather", a song I always think of as Dylan's perfect folk song – and which Dylan sings these days as if it is a folk song rather than his own creation - draws on this same tradition. The first two verses set up the contrast between material possessions and the love professed in the song:

Oh, I'm sailin' away my own true love,
I'm sailin' away in the morning.
Is there something I can send you from across the sea,
From the place that I'll be landing?

No, there's nothin' you can send me, my own true love,
There's nothin' I wish to be ownin'.
Just carry yourself back to me unspoiled,
From across that lonesome ocean

And so on throughout the song, as the material objects are piled up:

I just thought you might want something fine
Made of silver or of golden

And the diamonds from the deepest ocean

And, finally, the Spanish boots of Spanish leather are the gift desired when love is lost.

The beautiful and beautifully complex love song "Love Minus Zero/No Limit", released in 1965 on "Bringing it All Back Home", a song about which I write extensively through this book, introduces the love/money tension in a more hidden fashion. First there, is the title - an equation between love and numbers (you can't minus zero from love, and even if you did, it would still be love, because anything minus zero is itself; and what do you get when you divide love by no limit?) that is played out in the song:

People carry roses,
Make promises by the hours,
My love she laughs like the flowers,
Valentines can't buy her.

Of course valentines can't buy her, she's not for sale, unlike those people who carry roses. So the reference in the next stanza to "dime stores" takes us back to this same contrast between love and money:

In the dime stores and bus stations,
People talk of situations

And Dylan returns to the theme a final time in the last stanza:

Bankers' nieces seek perfection,
Expecting all the gifts that wise men bring.

It could have been anyone's nieces, but "bankers" and "gifts" reminds us that this is a song about the valueless of money when compared to love.

In Dylan's reworking of the theme on the jokey "Leopard Skin Pill Box Hat", from "Blonde on Blonde", the relationship is so shallow the "loves you for yourself/loves you for your money" theme goes one step backwards in a way that reveals Dylan's brilliant sense of humor:

Well, I see you got a new boyfriend
You know, I never seen him before
Well, I saw him
Makin' love to you
You forgot to close the garage door
You might think he loves you for your money
But I know what he really loves you for
It's your brand new leopard-skin pill-box hat

Love and money on "Blood on the Tracks"

As with most of the other themes in this book, it's that album of love lost, "Blood on the Tracks", which offers the most intense and consistent reflection of the tensions between love and money. As he reworked the album's lyrics Dylan tried to determine how he wanted to express the relationship between the two, in particular in different endings for "Idiot Wind" in the notebook in which he wrote the album's lyrics. As with most themes on the album, Dylan started with the first track, "Tangled up in Blue":

Her folks they said our lives together
Sure was gonna be rough
They never did like Mama's homemade dress
Papa's bankbook wasn't big enough.

It's not the size of Papa's bank book which is the problem of course, but the amount of money in it – the eternal problem when two folk get together from different social classes. The next reference comes in the same stanza:

And I was standin' on the side of the road
Rain fallin' on my shoes
Heading out for the East Coast
Lord knows I've paid some dues gettin' through,
Tangled up in blue.

The idea of paying dues for love is one that runs through the album. "Paying dues", originally related to paying to join a club or be part of a union, has come to mean paying for something you deserve.

There's a related theme in "Tangled up in Blue" concerning the need to make money:

I had a job in the Great North Woods
Working as a cook for a spell...

I lucky was to be employed
Working for a while on a fishing boat

She was working in a topless place

Then he started into dealing with slaves
And something inside of him died
She had to sell everything she owned
And froze up inside

Some are mathematicians, some are carpenters' wives

Mathematicians of course being the ultimate counters.

"Simple Twist of Fate" is an interesting song on love and money because it appears from Dylan's original recounting of this song in his notebook for "Blood on the Tracks" that the meeting wasn't one of chance, but a client who falls in love with a prostitute. It was originally called "4th Street Affair"; presumably this refers to 4th Street in Greenwich Village New York, which has a history of prostitution:[38]

> After 1880, Bleeker Street from the Bowery to Broadway was full of "numerous dives and other vile resorts in full blast." Describing East Fourth Street between Broadway and the Bowery, one irate resident said, "[G]ood citizens cannot return from the theatre late at night without having things snatched from their persons and being insulted by brazen faced street walkers!...[T]his street is a den of brazen women and pickpockets.".....Well into the twentieth century, residents complained about the many hotel and furnished-room house prostitutes who traversed Second and Third avenues."

The "canal" in the first line of the second verse then may refer to Canal Street, originally an old canal, and about a 15 minute walk from 4th Street.

Dylan had second thoughts about this and revised the song to take it closer to the theme of lost love

---

38   Gilfoyle, T. (1992): *City of Eros. New York City, Prostitution and the Commercialization of Sex 1790-1920.* W.W. Norton, 212-3. Dylan of course composed a song called "Positively 4th Street 10 years before "Simple Twist of Fate".

that haunts the album. In an original version in his notebook he wrote:

> *They stopped into a cheap motel*
> *With a broken (buzzing) light*[39]

Subsequently changed to:

> *And stopped into a strange hotel with a neon burnin' bright.*

The revision from "cheap" to "strange" is key; the former emphasizes money, while the latter emphasizes the confusion which is central to the released version of the song. The third verse is an interesting one too. In his notebook Dylan wrote:

> *A flute upon the corner played*
> *As she was walkin' by the arcade.*
> *As the light bust through a cut-up shade where he was wakin' up,*
> *She raised her weary head and couldn't help but hate*
> *Cashing in on a simple twist of fate*

We learn a little bit about the woman here – she has taken advantage of the man by "cashing in",

---

39   Dylan's handwriting isn't always easy to read, and there are many emendations in his notebook, giving lie to the idea that he composed spontaneously. For those interested, the notebook contains variations on several of the released songs, and lyrics for several songs which have perhaps never been recorded.

presumably payment for sex. But in the released version we hear:

> A saxophone someplace far off played
> As she was walkin' by the arcade.
> As the light bust through a beat-up shade where he was wakin' up,
> She dropped a coin into the cup of a blind man at the gate
> And forgot about a simple twist of fate.

The meaning is completely different – she simply, while dropping a coin into a cup, forgets about last night. But remnants of the idea of the women being a prostitute remain with the reference to the "coin". In Dylan's notebook for "Blood on the Tracks", the penultimate verse reads:

> Like an acrobat he does his stunt
> Then [illegible] he'll hunt
> Hunt her down by the waterfront
> Where the merchant ships all come in
> Maybe she'll pick him up again
> How long must he wait once more for a simple twist of fate.

"Pick him up" in the sense of picking someone up in a bar is changed in the released version to "pick him out". Pick him out again? From where? Grand Master of the Preposition, Dylan would not have made such a change unthinkingly.[40] Here is the released version:

> *He hears the ticking of the clocks*
> *And walks along with a parrot that talks,*
> *Hunts her down by the waterfront docks where the sailors all come in.*
> *Maybe she'll pick him out again, how long must he wait*
> *Once more for a simple twist of fate.*

The other interesting change in this verse is from "merchant ships" to "sailors". While merchant ships reminds us about the mercantile nature of the relationship, sailors remind us of the high levels of prostitution in dock areas to service ships stopping for a day or two. So, originally "Simple Twist of Fate" was a song about sex, love and money, and despite his revisions Dylan maintained the key theme of "Blood on the Tracks".

---

[40] As opposed to the "Master of the bluff and master of the proposition" on "Slow Train Coming". There's a similar change of preposition in the next song on the album, so that the words take on a completely different meaning, from:

I know that I can find you
In somebody's room

To:

I know where I can find you
In somebody's room.

But such changes are commonplace in Dylan's songs. My all-time favorite is from "Just Like a Women" where Dylan uses "as" rather than "by" when friends are being introduced.

The theme comes up again in the next two songs, first "You're a Big Girl Now":

Bird on the horizon
Sitting on the fence
He's singing his song for me
At his own expense

You have to be Bob Dylan to come up with a rhyme like "fence/expense", but the point here is that the "expense" in these compressed lines take us back to "paying dues" in "Tangled up in Blue" and on to a later stanza of the song:

I know that I can find you
In somebody's room
It's a price I have to pay
You're a big girl all the way

Dylan choice of this financial imagery is the perfect contrast between lost love (ever present in this song) and money.

On to "Idiot Wind", the album's discordant track, which is as much about blame and hatred as lost love. We are immediately back to money in the first stanza:

They say I shot a man called Gray
And took his wife to Italy
She inherited a million bucks

And when she died it came to me
I can't help it if I'm lucky

In Dylan's notebook for "Blood on the Tracks" he originally wrote "three million bucks" – perhaps "a million bucks" sang better?

There are three different endings to this song in Dylan's notebook. Here is the ending as released:

I been double-crossed now for the very last time
and now I'm finally free,
I kissed goodbye the howling beast on the bor-
derline which separated you from me.
You'll never know the hurt I suffered nor the pain
I rise above,
And I'll never know the same about you, your
holiness or your kind of love,
And it makes me feel so sorry.

It may make him feel sorry but he certainly isn't saying "sorry". In a song full of hatred it's odd to end on a line like "your holiness or your kind of love". In the version recorded for the New York City "Blood on the Tracks" sessions in September 1974, Dylan sang a different ending:

You close your eyes and part your lips
And slip your fingers from your glove
You can have the best there is
But it's gonna cost ya all your love
You won't get it for money

Why the change? Too much pomposity in "You can have the best there is"? Or too obvious a contrast between love and money?

Dylan's "Blood on the Tracks" notebook shows that he was trying to work out how he wanted to use the love versus money traditions. There are two alternate endings, with a variation in the first:

> *Scarlet (Blonde) hair, crimson lips, fingers fitting in a glove*
> *It would be nice to work it out, but we would have to do it for love*
> *Let's not do it for (the) money*
> *(We couldn't do it for money)*

And here is the second alternate ending:

> *We could change the world with space and time*
> *Space is place and God is love*
> *And time is money*

"Sorry" might be a better word to end the song than "money", but the traditions Dylan is drawing upon – the common poetic denominator in this case - was the contrast between eternal love and transitory money.

The same theme appears on other parts of the album, but mainly through passing references. Just to remind us that love needs to be earned for a price and at an expense, the next song, "Meet me in the Morning" includes:

Honey, you know I've earned your love.[41]

"Lily, Rosemary and the Jack of Hearts" is the album's odd song out, taking us to the wild west, card playing, a tale of a perfect bank robbery and a dancer falling in love with an outlaw, full of references to money, but with little to say about love.[42]

Dylan returns to money one last time on the album on "Shelter from the Storm":

> *In a little hilltop village, they gambled for my clothes*
> *I bargained for salvation an' they gave me a lethal dose.*
> *I offered up my innocence and got repaid with scorn.*
> *"Come in," she said,*
> *"I'll give you shelter from the storm."*

Why did Dylan consistently have the contrast between money and love on his mind when he was writing "Blood on the Tracks", in a way in which it isn't covered in his work before or since? Perhaps

---

41   Only four lines from Dylan's notebook were kept for the released song:
Look at the sun sinkin' like a ship
Look at the sun sinkin' like a ship
Ain't that just like my heart, babe
When you kissed my lips?
42   "gambling wheel/Lily called another bet/he owned the town's only diamond mine/silver cane/precious as a child/and cleaned out the bank safe/it's said they got off with quite a haul"

because this literary theme is one that deals with betrayal, different values, and the power of human love and loss. But one other interesting thing about the album is, despite all the references to money, he never uses the actual word in any of the songs.

Like ice, like fire

Fire, as a representation of the passions of love, is as ancient as literature. We use various synonyms for love – ardour, flame, warmth. So when Dylan writes in "Love Minus Zero/No Limit":

> *My love she speaks like silence,*
> *Without ideals or violence,*
> *She doesn't have to say she's faithful,*
> *Yet she's true, like ice, like fire.*

Fire at least is recognizable as term of endearment, but ice? How true is ice – given that it tends to melt and has for a long time been a representation of coldness and hatred? And how true is fire, given its proximity to ice? Is Dylan having us on?

One of the best known North American poems is organized around the contrast between ice and fire, Robert Frost's "Fire and Ice", published in 1923, which equates fire and desire, and ice with hate:

> *Some say the world will end in fire,*
> *Some say in ice.*
> *From what I've tasted of desire*

> *I hold with those who favor fire.*
> *But if it had to perish twice,*
> *I think I know enough of hate*
> *To say that for destruction ice*
> *Is also great*
> *And would suffice.*

The tradition of using these two terms together has a much longer history, for example the sixteenth century English poet Edmund Spenser's "My love is like to ice", sonnet 30 in the poem "Amorett" composed in 1595:

> *My love is like to ice, and I to fire:*
> *How comes it then that this her cold so great*
> *Is not dissolved through my so hot desire,*
> *But harder grows the more I her entreat?*
> *Or how comes it that my exceeding heat*
> *Is not allayed by her heart-frozen cold,*
> *But that I burn much more in boiling sweat,*
> *And feel my flames augmented manifold?*
> *What more miraculous thing may be told,*
> *That fire, which all things melts, should harden ice,*
> *And ice, which is congeal'd with senseless cold,*
> *Should kindle fire by wonderful device?*
> *Such is the power of love in gentle mind,*
> *That it can alter all the course of kind.*

We might just pause on one other example, from Puccini's unfinished opera "Tunradot", first performed in 1926. In the second act of the opera Tunradot asks her suitor prince three riddles, the third of which is: *Gelo che ti da foco* - "What is like ice, but burns like fire?" – the answer being, of course, Tunradot the ice maiden who has enflamed the Prince's passion.

Fire and ice, heat and cold, reappear in different forms on "Blood on the Tracks" – not surprising perhaps given that the album deals with the heat of passion and the cold despair of lost love. We will see throughout this book how densely packed the imagery of "Blood on the Tracks" is – the road and the traveller, the bird, books and writing, love and money all weave their way through the songs pulling them into a tight and coherent whole, and referring us back to Dylan's many other uses of these themes as well as their importance in literature and music. Here we'll take a look at how he uses heat and cold as one code on the album.

The scene is set by the title of the opening song – "Tangled up in Blue" – and the contrast between blueness or coldness and the sun rising and the woman's red hair.[43] We come back to heat in the fifth verse, with a burner being lit on the stove and the words pouring off of the page like burning coal. In contrast to this burning in the next verse we have:

---

43   Red hair in literature and art sometimes suggests prostitution, for example representations of Mary Magdalene with long red hair. Scobie (p. 241) comments on the use of the colours red and blue in Dylan's movie "Renaldo and Clara": "But "Blue" also keys the color coding of the film: the concert sequences are all shot with a strong visual emphasis on red and blue."

> *Then he started into dealing with slaves*
> *And something inside of him died.*
> *She had to sell everything she owned*
> *And froze up inside.*

"Simple Twist of Fate", which follows so cleverly after "Tangled up in Blue" in theme and imagery, brings us back to the heat of passion in the first two verses with the references to a spark and the neon burnin' bright:

> *They sat together in the park*
> *As the evening sky grew dark,*
> *She looked at him and he felt a spark tingle to his bones.*

> *And stopped into a strange hotel with a neon burnin' bright.*
> *He felt the heat of the night hit him like a freight train*
> *Moving with a simple twist of fate.*

But, almost immediately, we return to passion's opposite:

> *Felt an emptiness inside to which he just could not relate*

There's more burning on "Idiot Wind" – the "lighting that might strike", the "smoke pouring out of a box-car door" and the burning building. And once again we return to the opposite on "If You See Her Say Hello":

We had a falling-out, like lovers often will
And to think of how she left that night, it still brings
me a chill

Now, enough about love, money and sex, intrepid reader. We hope you found this chapter entertaining, and that you will listen to "Blonde on Blonde", *including* the fourth side of the album, with new interest. Now is the time to travel deeper in Dyland, and delve into the world of Mr. Dylan's writing about writing.

CHAPTER 3

Poisoning him with words?

In Scorcese's movie of Dylan's "formative" years, "Don't Look Back", there's an apparently unrehearsed scene where Dylan stands in front of a store in London in May 1966.[44] He goes through a series of stream of consciousness joke poems, amusing himself at speed with extraordinary mental agility, using the billboards outside the two stores to create the poems. The billboards read:

Collect, clip, bath and return your dog
KNI 7727
Cigarettes and tobacco

Animals and birds bought or sold on commission

---

[44]   Tracked down to a store on the corner of Queen's Gate Mews, south of Kensington Gardens, and probably May 10 1966 – one piece of autobiographical information I had to include.
http://blogs.telegraph.co.uk/christopher_howse/blog/2008/05/18/bob_dylan_connections_in_london

Dylan's spontaneous poems go something like this:

I want a dog that's going to collect and clean my bath, return my cigarette and give tobacco to my animals and give my bird some commission

I'm looking for somebody to sell my dog collect my clip buy my animal and straighten out my bird

I'm looking for a place to bathe my bird, buy my dog, collect my clip sell me cigarettes and commission my bath

I'm looking for a place that's going to collect my commission, sell my dog, burn my bird and sell me some cigarettes

Burn my bonnet (?), collect my will, and bathe my commission

I'm looking for a place that's going to animal my soul, mitt my return, bathe my foot and collect my dog

Commission me to sell my animal to the bird that clips and buy my bath and turn me back to the cigarette

Is there anything this guy can't do with words? Is this Dylan just having fun, or an example of Dylan's writing style and surrealistic use of language at the time – the jumbled, piled-up imagery of "Blonde on Blonde", "Highway 61 Revisited" and "Bringing it All Back Home", playing with adverbs and nouns as adjectives – "Obviously Five Believers, Absolutely Sweet Marie, With Your Mercury Mouth in the Missionary Times" – to the point where it seems like any word will fit with any other if it sounds good? Is the point – language is arbitrary? Is it all about reciting the alphabet (a phrase from "Desolation Row") – sounds, yes, but meaning, perhaps? Or is it about words that come from the heart? Boucher includes an apt quote from Lorca as to the meaning of his poetry:

> There is a clarity that is perceived by the heart and clarity is perceived by the mind. You know, clarity is not a fixed idea. Sometimes something that is clear to the heart needs quite complex expression. You just let the words or tune speak to you and it's very clear. You give yourself to the kiss of the embrace and while it is going on there's not any need to know what is going on. You just dissolve into it….but if there is an obscurity in my work, it's something that no one can penetrate, not even me…You just try to be faithful to that interior landscape that has its own rules, its own mechanisms, and it's important to be faithful to them.[45]

But if words come from the heart, how are we to interpret them, and to know if they have any

---

45   Boucher, D. (2005) *Dylan and Cohen. Poets of Rock and Roll*. New York: Continuum, 162.

meaning deeper than the marks they make on the page?

Dylan's writing about creation and communication is central to many of his songs, not just those of the mid-60s; and his take on language is the focus this chapter. First I'll look at the way he writes about the difficulties or impossibility of communication, and other writers who have "expressed" the same thing. Then at how Dylan uses letters, books, and references to the written word in his songs, and what this says about Dylan as a writer, and his ambivalence towards writing. Then, how he uses the wind as an image of creativity, another tradition used by western poets. And last at the image of the bird as a representation of the artist, where Dylan draws on one of the most persistent common poetic denominators.

And you want somebody you don't have to speak to

For someone who makes his living by communicating, Dylan is pretty consistent about how difficult it is to communicate. In many of his songs it just isn't really worth striking up a conversation, as no-one has much to say.

As early as 1963, in "Don't Think Twice, It's All Right", Dylan is already writing about this:

Still I wish there was somethin' you would do or say
To try and make me change my mind and stay

We never did too much talkin' anyway
So don't think twice, it's all right

It ain't no use in callin' out my name, gal
Like you never did before
It ain't no use in callin' out my name, gal
I can't hear you any more

"We never did too much talkin' anyway" just about sums it up, as does the quote from "Queen Jane Approximately" from which the title of this section comes. Here's a few examples from Dylan's work about how it's better just to keep your mouth shut. I could have quoted more but in the spirit of not trying too hard to communicate this point I've restricted myself:

I'm a-singin' you the song, but I can't sing enough,
'Cause there's not many men that done the things that you've done.

I got my dark sunglasses, I'm carryin' for good luck my black tooth.
Don't ask me nothin' about nothin', I just might tell you the truth.

It's a restless hungry feeling
That don't mean no one no good,
When ev'rything I'm a-sayin'
You can say it just as good.

So now as I'm leavin'
I'm weary as Hell
The confusion I'm feelin'
Ain't no tongue can tell

Outside a rambling store-front window
Cats meowed to the break of day
Me, I kept my mouth shut, too
To you I had no words to say

There's no use in talking
And there's no need for blame

I thought you'd never say hello she said
You look like the silent type

I muttered something underneath my breath

Not a word was spoke between us, there was lit-
tle risk involved

Broken words never meant to be spoken

And the words that are used
For to get the ship confused
Will not be understood as they're spoken.

When she said "don't waste your words, they're
just lies"
I cried she was deaf

What's the matter with me,
I don't have much to say

Think I'll go out and go for a walk,
Not much happenin' here, nothin' ever does.
Besides, if she wakes up now, she'll just want me to talk
I got nothin' to say, 'specially about whatever was.

I ain't too good at conversation, girl,
So you might not know exactly how I feel

Our conversation was short and sweet

There was little to say, there was no conversation

I heard ten thousand whisperin' and nobody listenin'

Ain't talkin', just walkin'[46]

One of the interesting things about these quotes is that they cover Dylan's work from start to finish, from "Song to Woody" to "Ain't Talking". So what is it that Dylan is trying to tell us, or not tell us. It's a familiar literary paradox, saying you've got nothing to say while saying something. It's saying that words, in the

---

46   "Song to Woody"; "Outlaw Blues"; " "One Too Many Mornings"; "With God On My Side"; "Temporary Like Achilles"; "Love is Just a Four Letter Word"; "Farewell Angelina" as sung on the Bootleg Series 1-3"; Tangled Up in Blue"; "Shelter from the Storm"; "Everything is Broken"; "When the Ship Comes In"; "Fourth Time Around"; "Watching the River Flow"; "Not Dark Yet"; "I and I"; "Don't fall apart on me tonight"; "You're a Big Girl Now"; "Day of the Locusts"; "11 Outlined Epitaths"; "A Hard Rain's A-Gonna Fall"; "Ain't Talkin' ".

end, are inadequate. Scobie has picked this up on one of Dylan's albums, "Time Out of Mind", but it's a theme which cuts right through:

> *this self-undermining of the singer's authority extends to repeated statements about the inefficacy of words, of the very act of speaking. "there are things I could say," he tells us, "but I don't". And later in the same song: "I see nothing to be gained by any explanation/There's no words that need to be said." The singer is "tired of talking, tired of trying to explain"…. And climatically in "Highlands": "The party's over and there's less and less to say." When he tells his lover to "seal up the book and not write any more", it might as well be himself that he is addressing.*[47]

On "Highlands" the creation has come down to drawing a few lines on a napkin at the request of a server in a restaurant in Boston, but even this sketch is disparaged.

Of all Dylan's albums, the one where words are most problematic is perhaps "Bringing it all Back Home", released in 1965. Three songs - "Gates of Eden", "It's Allright Ma (I'm Only Bleeding)" and "Love Minus Zero/No Limit" concentrate on the challenges of communicating. "Gates of Eden" includes some of Dylan's most impenetrable imagery, more sound than meaning perhaps, but part of the song is about

---

47   p. 297-8. Quotes are from "Standing in the Doorway"; "'Til I Fell in Love with You"; and "Tryin' to Get to Heaven".

language and sound: babies wailing, a savage soldier complaining to a shoeless hunter who's gone deaf, hound dogs baying, laughing at Utopian hermit monks, whispering in the wings, the lonesome sparrow singing, the grey flannel dwarf screaming, the princess and the prince discussing (what is real and what is not), and at the end of the song the telling of dreams:

> *At dawn my lover comes to me*
> *And tells me of her dreams*
> *With no attempts to shovel the glimpse*
> *Into the ditch of what each one means*
> *At times I think there are no words*
> *But these to tell what's true*
> *And there are no truths outside the Gates of Eden*

Interpretation of dreams is pointless, and there are "no words/But these to tell what's true" - the final self-referential comment, effectively meaning that there are no words at all. Back to the paradox – the writer is using the medium of a song to tell us that there's no point in trying to communicate.

"Love Minus Zero/No Limit" is equally a song about how much better silence is than false words, a song of contrasts - between speaking like silence and laughing like the flowers (neither presumably a particularly loud activity, my flowers laugh pretty quietly) and making promises by the hours; between speaking softly and talking of situations; and between repeating quotations and knowing too much to argue. Speaking like silence is a paradox reflected in an earlier piece by Dylan, the liner notes to "The Times They Are A-Changin' ":

> (you ask of love?
> there is no love
> except in silence
> an' silence doesn't say a word).

Dylan writes on "Love Minus Zero/No Limit":

> She doesn't have to say she's faithful,
> Yet she's true, like ice, like fire.

Actions speak louder than words? Perhaps. Dylan ups the ante on "Something There is About You" from "Planet Waves", released in 1974:

> I could say that I'd be faithful, I could say it in one sweet, easy breath
> But to you that would be cruelty and to me it surely would be death.

The phrase "Money doesn't talk it swears" has received attention as a Dylanism – an aphorism developed from a well-known saying and twisted to a different set of values. But "It's Alright, Ma (I'm Only Bleeding)" is also a song full of negativity about communication:

> Suicide remarks are torn
> From the fool's gold mouthpiece
> The hollow horn plays wasted words

Watch waterfalls of pity roar
You feel to moan but unlike before
You discover
That you'd just be
One more person crying.

So don't fear if you hear
A foreign sound to your ear
It's alright, Ma, I'm only sighing.

While others say don't hate nothing at all
Except hatred.

Disillusioned words like bullets bark

While preachers preach of evil fates

Advertising signs that con you
Into thinking you're the one

When a trembling distant voice, unclear
Startles your sleeping ears to hear.

Speak jealously of them that are free

Tell nothing except who to idolize
And then say God bless him.

While one who sings with his tongue on fire
Gargles in the rat race choir

"Wasted words", "waterfalls of pity roar", disillusioned words", "singing with a tongue on fire", money swearing –words just can't be trusted as a medium for communicating.

"Positively 4th Street", another of Dylan's songs with an adverb starting the title, is perhaps his most vindictive song about the falseness of speech. Ricks in his incisive analysis has pointed out the importance of "knowing" in the song, with "know" occurring seven times.[48] There's another theme, which is the falseness of saying. Whoever the person who has got a lotta nerve is, they're accused of false talking – see the italics in the lyrics:

You got a lotta nerve
To say you are my friend
When I was down
You just stood there grinning

You got a lotta nerve
To say you got a helping hand to lend
You just want to be on
The side that's winning

You say I let you down
You know it's not like that
If you're so hurt
Why then don't you show it

You say you lost your faith
But that's not where it's at

---

48 pp. 63-4.

You had no faith to lose
And you know it

I know the reason
That you talk behind my back
I used to be among the crowd
You're in with

Do you take me for such a fool
To think I'd make contact
With the one who tries to hide
What he don't know to begin with

You see me on the street
You always act surprised
You say, "How are you?" "Good luck"
But you don't mean it

When you know as well as me
You'd rather see me paralyzed
Why don't you just come out once
And scream it

Speaking falsely to screaming is a natural transition, because screaming isn't any kind of communication, which is why the off rhyme between "mean it" and "scream it" works so well, as screaming conveys no meaning.

The pattern is clear. Dylan songs are at best ambivalent about communication, as he plays with the paradox that he's telling us it's not worth saying anything.

Written in my soul?

Dylan is not alone when he writes about hollow horns playing wasted words. Western literature has at its heart a fascination with the creative process, and a fear of creativity and the written word. There is a reverence for literature past, manifesting itself in the many writers who have used their literary predecessors as sources. And there are many novels and poems that dwell on the creative act, and an equal number that include destruction of a book or a word as a central or hidden feature. Who wouldn't be scared of baring their soul to the world in a book? And if your job is to sit all day writing, wouldn't you eventually start writing about writing? But if the focus of the creative act is to write about the process and perhaps pointlessness of writing, doesn't that become a little self-referential – and, where's the point? Dylan draws on and is part of this tradition.

Dylan ambivalence about creating is perhaps most evident when he refers to the written word in his songs. Take that extraordinary, poignant and much admired and discussed lost love song, "Boots of Spanish Leather", released in 1964, which I already discussed from the angle of money and love in the last chapter. Ricks includes a brilliant analysis of its cadences, rhymes and rhythms, and Gray reveals its heritage in traditional British folk ballads, particularly "Gypsey Davy" which was perhaps written at the beginning of the eighteenth century.[49] But the

---

49   Gray, pp. 657-6; http://en.wikipedia.org/wiki/The_Gypsy_Laddie

key element of the song is that, after refusing any gifts from his (or her) love, what is received is a letter:

I got a letter on a lonesome day,
It was from her ship a-sailin',
Saying I don't know when I'll be comin' back again,
It depends on how I'm a-feelin'.

And there's an interesting echo of this letter when the song comes to its last word – "leather".

Hope you never get a letter from Dylan, because letters in his songs are almost always bad news. The written word brings no good. Just as well in "Man With the Long Black Coat": "She never left nothing, not even a note".

Take the regret in the last lines of "Idiot Wind":

Idiot wind, blowing through the buttons of our coats,
Blowing through the letters that we wrote.
Idiot wind, blowing through the dust upon our shelves,
We're idiots, babe.
It's a wonder we can even feed ourselves.

Or take "Not Dark Yet" from the 1997 album "Time Out of Mind". There's also been a lot of discussion about this song. Ricks draws parallels to Keats' "Ode to a Nightingale", and several authors talk about the song in relation to Dylan's near fatal illness at the time. But, like "Boots of Spanish Leather", it's a song which turns on the sending of a letter:

> *Well my sense of humanity has gone down the drain*
> *Behind every beautiful thing there's been some kind of pain*
> *She wrote me a letter and she wrote it so kind*
> *She put down in writing what was in her mind*
> *I just don't see why I should even care*
> *It's not dark yet, but it's getting there*[50]

Considering it's getting pretty dark out there, we have to assume that what was in that letter was not good news. The fact that "Time out of Mind" is an album partly about lost love only adds to this view.

Then there's the song which starts with a postcard and passports (different kinds of "literary" mediums), has Einstein reciting the alphabet, cards that read "Have Mercy on his Soul", Casanova poisoned with words, and which ends with another letter:

> *Yes, I received your letter yesterday*
> *(About the time the door knob broke)*
> *When you asked how I was doing*

---

50   Alex Ross in "The Wanderer" in B. Hedin (ed) "Studio A: The Bob Dylan Reader", New York: Norton, 2004, p. 309 writes "Time of out Mind" is thrillingly Dylanish, because he has returned with a vengeance to the magpie mode of writing. Old song: "she wrote me a letter and she wrote it so kind,/And in this letter these words you can find." Unfortunately Ross doesn't provide details of the "old song" from which he is quoting, and I haven't been able to trace it.

Was that some kind of joke?
All these people that you mention
Yes, I know them, they're quite lame
I had to rearrange their faces
And give them all another name
Right now I can't read too good
Don't send me no more letters no
Not unless you mail them
From Desolation Row

The ending of "Desolation Row" has always seemed mysterious. This is a song without a beginning, in that it doesn't tell a linear story, but rather is a series of vignettes linked by desolation row – whatever that is. It's a song which could have gone on and on, at least until Dylan ran out of his cast of characters, which would be never. So why end on a letter, not being able to read too good, and not wanting any more letters? Why not end on another literary character. Perhaps to complete the circle from the post-card to the letter, and to point out the meaningless of the written word?[51]

Many novels, poems and songs include letters as key plot elements, and there is a genre of episto-lary novels and more recently novels written as blogs and emails. There is also a Blues influence, for example a version of "Corrina, Corrina" which

---

51   Dylan plays a clever game with "yes" and "no" in this stanza, starting two lines with "yes", punning on "know", and including "no" as the last rhyme – having already used "know" as a rhyme in an earlier stanza.

Dylan rewrote for his second album, as well as songs sung by Blind Willie McTell, Blind Lemon Jefferson, Son House ("Death Letter"), Skip James (in "Special Rider Blues", which refers to the news of the death of a loved one through a letter), Robert Johnson, and Muddy Waters ("Sad Letter Blues") all of whom we know influenced Dylan enormously. Springsteen uses the same technique in a few songs, including "Livin' in the Future" and "Brilliant Disguise". Here are the lyrics of the traditional "Corrine, Corinna":

Corrine Corinna: what's the matter now
You didn't write no letter: you didn't love me no how
Goodbye Corinna : and it's fare thee well
When I'm coming back babe: can't nobody tell

Then there are the numerous (and often sentimental) soldiers' last letter home, usually to their mothers, from the war front, for example "Soldier's Last Letter", recorded by Texan country singer Ernest Tubb in 1941, where the postman delivers a letter which fills the mother's heart with joy, until she realizes it is the last letter she will receive from her son.

Dylan wrote his own version of the sad soldier's letter home in "Cross the Green Mountain", for the movie "Gods and Generals" which was released in 2003:

A letter to mother came today
Gun shot wound to the breast is what it did say.
But he'll be better soon, he's on a hospital bed
But he'll never be better, he's already dead.

Many people hearing this song would recognize the tradition and could picture the bereaved mother holding the crumpled letter to her heart.

Dylan also recorded the Bluegrass song "Two Soldiers", on "World Gone Wrong" in 1993, a song from the American civil war much collected in the Southern Appalachians which has the same theme[52]:

But if you ride back and I am left,
You'll do as much for me,
Mother, you know, must hear the news,
So write to her tenderly…

There's no one to write to the blue-eyed girl
The words that her lover had said.
Momma, you know, awaits the news,
And she'll only know he's dead.

Dylan comes from a generation where the arrival of the written word was more than likely bad news. As Steinbeck wrote: "Even I can remember when a telegram meant just one thing – a death in the family."[53]

Like letters, speech and communication, "words" denote negative experience in Dylan's songs. I've included a few example in the first section of this

---

52   http://www.bobdylanroots.com/two.html
53   John Steinbeck. *Travels with Charley. In Search of America*. p. 102. New York: The Viking Press. 1962.

chapter. Dylan also writes about broken words ("Everything is Broken"), "Fast Fading Words" ("Eternal Circle"), swear words and snarling ("The Lonesome Death of Hattie Carroll"), "mind-polluting words" ("Million Miles"), and love being just a four letter word.

As well as including letters in his songs, Dylan engages in various forms of meta-fiction, or references to story-telling or the creative process within the story. Like letters, or conversations, books don't cut it:

> *You've been with the professors*
> *And they've all liked your looks*
> *With great lawyers you have*
> *Discussed lepers and crooks*
> *You've been through all of*
> *F. Scott Fitzgerald's books*
> *You're very well read*
> *It's well known*

> *I can't feel you anymore, I can't even touch the books you've read*
> *Every time I crawl past your door, I been wishin' I was somebody else instead.*

> *In the dime stores and bus stations,*
> *People talk of situations,*
> *Read books, repeat quotations,*
> *Draw conclusions on the wall.*

> *The geometry of innocent flesh on the bone*
> *Causes Galileo's math book to get thrown.*

Don't show me no picture show or give me no book to read,
It don't satisfy the hurt inside nor the habit that it feeds.

In the courtroom of honor, the judge pounded his gavel
To show that all's equal and that the courts are on the level
And that the strings in the books ain't pulled and persuaded[54]

It's interesting Dylan should be so condescending to a book in the last quote, from "The Lonesome Death of Hattie Carroll". Of course, the strings in the books are pulled and persuaded, just like the ladder of law has a top and a bottom, like every ladder. But it's an odd use of "book" here, because books don't usually have strings in them – strings can be pulled (but not usually persuaded, and how do you persuade a string in a book?). This perhaps refers to the "sentence" which ends the last line of the song – as usual Dylan doesn't miss a trick (or two). Not only that, but earlier in this song, the cops "booked" William Zanzinger for first-degree murder.

There is one reference to a book which at first seems positive, from "Tangled up in Blue":

54   "Ballad of a Thin Man"; "Idiot Wind"; "love Minus Zero/No Limit"; "Tombstone Blues"; "Shot of Love" ; "The Lonesome Death of Hattie Carroll".

Then she opened up a book of poems
And handed it to me
Written by an Italian poet
From the thirteenth century.
And every one of them words rang true
And glowed like burnin' coal
Pourin' off of every page
Like it was written in my soul from me to you,
Tangled up in blue.

As I noted in chapter 2, the images of fire, heat and burning which are common in "Blood on the Tracks", and to which I return in Chapter 4, are not necessarily positive – having something written in your soul with a heat like burning coal sounds kind of painful. There's another kind of book which is contrasted in the first verse of this song:

Her folks they said our lives together
Sure was gonna be rough
They never did like Mama's homemade dress
Papa's bankbook wasn't big enough.

The bankbook (which today seems so anachronistic but previously was used for recording bank deposits), representing money and the status it can bring, and the book of poems, representing (presumably) love, summarise beautifully the contrast between these two dominant themes of western literature, another major theme in Dylan's work which I covered in the last chapter.

Dylan also engages in a kind of meta-fiction not available to poets or novelists – references to musical instruments and the sound of that instrument at the same time, as in "Joey" where he sings the line: "Opened up his eyes to the tune of an accordion" while an accordion plays, but there are numerous references to other musical instruments – drums, horns, guitars (playing as skirts sway), harmonicas (playing the skeleton keys) in "Visions of Johanna", one of several songs which focus on musical instruments as a symbol of the muse. Musical instruments draw together the songs of "Blonde on Blonde", for they are present in almost every song – the guitar in "Rainy Day Women #12 &35", the harmonica in "Visions of Johanna", the drums and trumpet in "Absolutely Sweet Marie", the drums in "Sad Eyed Lady of the Lowlands", the organ, saxophones, bells, horns, and flute in "I Want You", and so on.

Similarly he constantly draws attention to his own singing. His first publicly released self-written song, "Song to Woody", contains the line:

I'm a singin' you the song, but I can't sing enough.

Well, it is a song to Woody, so you'd expect Dylan to be singing it – but do we really need three reminders of that in one line? But Dylan can't help bringing up the fact that he's signing in his songs. "I know my song well before I start singing", he sings in "A Hard Rain's A-Gonna Fall"; and just as well, for Dylan's lyrics are some of the most complicated around. How could anyone remember the lyrics to "Vision of Johanna"? "Leavin' nobody to sing his sad song" he sings in "Only a Hobo" – but hold on, isn't Dylan singing his sad song for him; "Ev'rybody singin' a sorrowful tune" he sorrowfully sings in "Oxford Town"; "Suddenly I found you and the spirit in me sings" the spirit in him sings in "Something There is About You."

Meta-fiction is a key tradition in western literature. A marvellous representative is Sterne's ":Tristam Shandy". Don Quixote becomes obsessed with books of chivalry. Chaucer's "Canterbury Tales" and Boccaccio's "The Decameron" are early storytelling within stories. "Pride and Prejudice" is a novel which includes a large number of letters. In Chaucer's "Book of the Duchess" the narrator reads Ovid's tale of Ceyx and Alcyone, which mirrors his own. Shakespeare's play within a play in "Hamlet" has the same effect. There are numerous novels about a writer creating a story (McEwan's "Atonement" is a recent one), novels about readers reading a novel (for example Calvino's "If on a Winter's Night a Traveler"), and novels within novels, such as Gaarder's "Sophie's World".

Writers love drawing attention to themselves writing, both to point out how clever they are, but also to establish that what they are creating is fiction, not life. As Gabriel Josipovici, an astute critic of postmodernism, has argued:

The modern novel draws attention to the rules which govern its creation in order to force the reader into recognising that it is not the world....The *trompe-l'oeil* effects of modern art...the playful inversion of the novel form and the parody of language and convention in modern fiction....[make] us realise with a shock that we are dealing not with the world but with one more object in the world, one made by a human being.[55]

As many have pointed out, Dylan's songs are full of literary references and borrowings. Gray in particular has documented how Dylan has borrowed from the Blues, from movies, and from nursery rhymes. When he does this Dylan is doing three things. First he is acknowledging his lexicon, as he called it, the many writers and singers who have influenced and moved him. Second he is shoring up his own personal world, pulling together the many fragments that have given him meaning – as Eliot put it in "The Waste Land": "These fragments I have shored against my ruins". Increasingly over the last 20 years Dylan's songs have appeared as fragments brought together to make up songs which have no clear narrative voice and no clear storyline, but instead are a number of allusions forced together into a song – the songs on "Time Out of Mind"," "Love and Theft" " and "Modern Times" certainly fit into this category, with their multiple references to masters old and recent.[56] And third he is pointing out as many writers before him have done that what he is doing is creating and playing, our most elemental acts.

---

55   Gabriel Josipovici (1971) *The World and the Book. A Study of Modern Fiction.* Stanford: Stanford University Press.
56   See Polito and Thomas.

But if there is one literary tradition that values the written word and books and music from the past, there is an equally strong tradition that denigrates the written word and not only closes the pages on the text but destroys it. There's a sense that telling something is itself destructive, as in Blake's fragment "Never seek tell thy love":

> Never seek to tell thy love,
> Love that never told can be;
> For the gentle wind does move,
> Silently, invisibly.

> I told my love, I told my love,
> I told her all my heart;
> Trembling, cold, in ghastly fears,
> Ah! she doth depart.

The telling is the tragedy which makes love depart. This more negative literary tradition deals with the impossibility of writing, the loss of the muse, and where self-reference to a book within a book often involves the trashing or degrading of a book, a page of a book, a letter or a word, denigrating the whole creative act. The fear of writing comes across in the immolation of the book as a kind of sacred ritual. Deep inside many books there are other books which can't escape and that the writer destroys. Creative writing can be an intensely self-reflective activity –is there anything more self-reflective? There are many many examples of books decaying within novels and plays, and here are a few. Conrad's

"The Secret Agent", from which Dylan borrowed for "Stuck Inside of Mobile", has on its first page:

> *The window contained photographs of more or less undressed dancing girls; nondescript packages in wrappers like patent medicines; closed yellow paper envelopes, very flimsy, and marked two-and-six in heavy black figures; a few numbers of ancient French comic publications hung across a string as if to dry; a dingy blue china bowl, a casket of black wood, bottles of marking ink, and rubber stamps; a few books, with titles hinting at impropriety; a few apparently old copies of obscure newspapers, badly printed, with titles like The Torch, The Gong - rousing titles.*

The photographs, yellow envelopes, French publications and old newspapers all point towards the decay towards which books veer.

The first part of "Don Quixote" has a scene in which the priest and the housekeeper of the knight go through the chivalry books that have turned him mad. In a kind of auto-da-fé they burn most of them. Then there's Bradbury's "Fahrenheit 451", where entire libraries are torched and which begins with the words:

> *It was a pleasure to burn…He wanted above all, like the old joke, to shove a marshmallow on a stick in the furnace, while the flapping pigeon-winged books died on the porch and lawn of*

the house. While the books went up in sparkling whirls and blew away on a wind turned dark with burning.

There's no surprise that in Nabokov's novel, "Pale Fire", there's a book burning reminiscent of Bradbury's, given Nabokov's penchant for meta-fiction (or perhaps hyper-fiction in his case): "I recall seeing [John Shade, the novel's 'hero'] from my porch, on a brilliant morning, burning a whole stack of [his drafts] in the pale fire of the incinerator before which he stood with bent head like an official mourner among the wind-borne black butterflies of that backyard auto-da-fé." The unwritten book by the Consul in Lowry's "Under the Volcano" (itself written on a beach not too far from where I write) is a great example of the failure of language. In that book letters remain unwritten or unmailed, and love is doomed by a postcard that travels the world before arriving 10 months late. In Oriana Fallaci's novel "The Man" the book's hero attempts to write a book but is unable to progress past page twenty three, and eventually destroys the hand written pages.

In Elias Canetti's novel "Auto-da-fé" Peter Klein, a Professor of immense learning, lives in a world of books about which he cares more than anything, and is forced by bumping into life (in the form of a wife whose main interest is getting control of his money) to leave his library and eventually his sanity. Before he does so he first turns all the spines of the volumes to the wall, talking to the volumes as he does so. He then carries the library around in his head, unpacking it each night. At the end of the novel Klein destroys his library:

The books cascade off the shelves on to the floor. He takes them up in his long arms. Very quietly, so that they can't hear him outside, he carried pile after pile into the hall. He builds them up high against the iron door. And while the frantic din tears his brain to fragments, he builds a mighty bulwark out of the books. The hall is filled with volume upon volume. He fetches the ladder to help him. Soon he has reached the ceiling. He goes back to his room. The shelves gape at him. In front of the writing desk the carpet is ablaze. He goes into the bedroom next to the kitchen and drags out all the old newspapers. He pulls the pages apart, and crumples them, he rolls them into balls, and throws them into all the corners. He places the ladder in the middle of the room where it stood before. He climbs up to the sixth step, looks down on the fire and waits.[57]

My final example, an elegant account of the book which destroys itself within a book, is Umberto Eco's "Name of the Rose". This medieval detective story is narrated by an old monk who as a young man was a disciple of William of Baskerville, who goes to a Benedictine monastery in Italy in the 14th century to investigate a murder. It has at its heart a library which

---

57   Canetti, E. (2000) *Auto-da-fé*. New York, Farrar, Strauss and Giroux, p. 464.

is also a labyrinth, kept by a blind librarian called Jorge of Burgos, itself a none too coy reference to the blind Argentinian story writer Jorge Luis Borges who wrote a book of short stories called "Labyrinths". At the end of the book the labyrinthine library, the "greatest library in Christendom", is burnt. Not only that, but the murders in the novel are caused by poison placed on the corners of an illegal volume which the librarian wants to hide, so that his victims poison themselves as they lick their fingers to turn the page. Not just any volume, but the lost second volume of Aristotle's "Poetics" on comedy. What better example could there be of "poisoning him with words", the fate of one of the characters in Dylan's "Desolation Row":

> They're spoonfeeding Casanova
> To get him to feel more assured
> Then they'll kill him with self-confidence
> After poisoning him with words

And what better example of the self-referential text that turns in on itself. When caught by the detective monk, the old blind librarian Burgos commits suicide by eating pages of book he has poisoned:

> He spoke, and with his fleshless, diaphanous hands he began slowly tearing to strips and shreds the limp pages of the manuscript, stuffing them into his mouth, slowly swallowing them as if he were consuming the host and he wanted to make it flesh of his flesh.[58]

---

58   Umberto Eco (1984) "The Name of the Rose" London: Pan Books, p. 480.

The ensuing fight over the book leads to a lamp being broken and the burning of the library. Years later the narrator returns to the library:

> *Along one stretch of wall I found a bookcase, still miraculously erect, having come through the fire I cannot say how; it was rotted by water and consumed by termites. In it there were still a few pages. Other remnants I found by rummaging in the ruins below…Some fragments of parchment had faded, others permitted the glimpse of an image's shadow, or the ghost of one or more words. At times I found pages where whole sentences were legible; more often, intact bindings, protected by what had once been metal studs…Ghosts of books, apparently intact on the outside but consumed within; yet sometimes a half page had been saved, an incipit was discernible, a title….At the end of my patient reconstruction, I had before me a kind of lesser library, a symbol of the greater vanished one: a library made up of fragments, quotations, unfinished sentences, amputated stumps of books.*[59]

Dylan is not alone in his suspicions of words and books. But before we close the book on the pages and the text (because I hope we care what happens next), here are some further thoughts on Dylan and words.[60]

---

59   Eco, p. 500.
60   "I'm closin' the book

On the pages and the text

20 pounds of headlines stapled to his chest?

One of the literary characters Dylan may refer to in "Desolation Row" is Franz Kafka – the reference being to Kafka's novel "The Castle" and Kafka's employment in an insurance company - the song certainly has an absurdist and Kafkaesque feel about it[61]:

> Now at midnight all the agents
> And the superhuman crew
> Come out and round up everyone
> That knows more than they do
> Then they bring them to the factory
> Where the heart-attack machine
> Is strapped across their shoulders
> And then the kerosene
> Is brought down from the castles
> By insurance men who go
> Check to see that nobody is escaping
> To Desolation Row

Kafka wrote another story, about literary tattooing, called "The Penal Colony". This is a weird story, even for Kafka. It stars a Traveller and an Officer, the former having responded to an invitation to an island colony to witness the execution of a soldier (the Condemned Man) condemned for disobeying

---

And I don't really care
What happens next."
"Going, Going, Gone"
61   Gray, pp. 138-9.

and insulting his superior. Dylan is not beyond using such generic names, especially in his liner notes and "Tarantula". In Kafka's story, the law which a condemned man has violated is inscribed on his body by a harrow (an agricultural instrument for tilling the soil, and from which we get the adjective "harrowing"). In other words, inscribed to death – which says something about Kafka's attitudes to words, and why he reputedly asked for all of his works to be destroyed. This makes Dylan's line in "Tangled up in Blue" – "Like it was written in my soul" – a little more sinister.

There a similar writing on the body (as opposed to the soul) in "Stuck Inside of Mobile with the Memphis Blues Again":

> *Now the preacher looked so baffled*
> *When I asked him why he dressed*
> *With twenty pounds of headlines*
> *Stapled to his chest.*

This post-modernist literary nightmare is shared by many authors, past and modern. The writer is condemned to write, but the writing itself never fully satisfies the needs of expression.

Blowing in the wind?

Let's move on from words and letters to other customary symbols of writing and poetic common denominators and how Dylan uses these. "Wind" is a key symbol in romantic poetry, a tradition from which Dylan borrowed extensively. In his book on English romanticism, Abrams writes:

> *That the poetry of Coleridge, Wordsworth, Shelley, Byron should be so thoroughly ventilated is itself noteworthy; but the surprising thing is how often, in the major poems, the wind is not only a property of the landscape, but also a vehicle for radical changes in the poet's mind. The rising wind, usually linked with the outer transition from winter to spring, is correlated with a complex subjective process: the return to a sense of community after isolation, the renewal of life and emotional vigour after apathy and a deathlike torpor, and an outburst of creative power following a period of imaginative sterility.*[62]

Dylan's "Lay Down Your Weary Tune", written around 1964, is a sweet example of the link from nature to music, related to movement towards vitality:

> *Struck by the sounds before the sun,*
> *I knew the night had gone.*
> *The morning breeze like a bugle blew*
> *Against the drums of dawn.*

In this song, it's the wind that's doing the listening:

> *The last of leaves fell from the trees*
> *And clung to a new love's breast.*

---

62   Abrams, M.H. (1984) *The Correspondent Breeze. Essays on English Romanticism*. New York: W.W. Norton, pp. 25-6).

The branches bare like a banjo played
To the winds that listened best.

And it's water that's humming like a harp:

I gazed down in the river's mirror
And watched its winding strum.
The water smooth ran like a hymn
And like a harp did hum.

But the effect on the singer is clear – the night has gone, and: "I stood unwound beneath the skies." – Abrams comments on the romantic poets that the wind led to the renewal of life and emotional vigour.

Dylan chose a different image in this song to the one used by the romantic poets. In these poets, Abrams argues, the wind usually sounds through a wind harp, which is a metaphor for the creator, with the wind, like breath, bringing inspiration:

Poetic man, in a statement by Shelley, which had close parallels in Coleridge and Wordsworth, is an instrument subject to impressions "like the alternations of an ever-changing wind over an Aeolian lyre which move it by their motion to every-changing melody." The wind-harp has become a persistent Romantic analogue of the poetic mind, the figurative mediator between outer motion and inner motion.[63]

---

63   Abrams, p.26. The link between wind and inspiration is nothing new. Dylan of course is famous for playing another kind of harp, the harmonica - also known as a harp:

So what about Dylan's song, "Blowin' in the Wind"? Why did he choose the wind as an image – is this a reference to the powers of creation? Dunlap has this to say about the song:

> *Despite Dylan's explanation, the phrase "blowin' in the wind" appears to mean more than just change may come eventually. Dylan's phrasing implies a teleological view of history; that is, civilization is moving purposefully towards a particular goal. However, unlike the theoretical inevitability of a Marxist-styled revolution with rules that one could articulate, the changes that Dylan foresees are discernible only through one's intuition. Special knowledge of the natural inevitability of*

In many parts of the American South, the harmonica is called *mouth harp*, *French harp* or just plain *harp*. The term is partly inspired by the *Aeolian harp*, a stringed instrument that is left outdoors to be played by the wind, whose name was taken from Aeolus, the god of the wind. Early names for the harmonica were Aeolina *Aeolian* and *Mund-Aeoline*, which stressed this link with the Aeolian harp. As the earliest harmonica-like instruments were little more than a few reeds attached to a reedplate that was held to the players lips, the resemblance to a harp was quite pronounced. The introduction to *Instructions for the Aeolina, or Mund-Harmonica*, published in New York in 1830 proudly boast:

THE AEOLINA from the originality of its construction and the beauty of its effects, is a decided novelty in the musical art; the expressive sweetness of its tones, the richness of the harmonies it renders, and the contrasts of its exulting swells and dying cadences, realize the poetical descriptions of the harp of Aeolus and greatly surpass its practical results; while the regularity of its scale gives it advantages of the most important kind, which that instrument does not possess. From the close resemblance of its tones to those of this harp of the winds and from the analogous circumstances under which the sound is produced in both instances, the name of the Aeolina has been derived.

http://www.patmissin.com/ffaq/q3.html

change would connect the sensibility of Dylan's song with the kind of access to a universal spirit or over-soul that informed Emerson's philosophy.[64]

But if the answer to all the questions that the song poses is "Blowin' in the Wind", doesn't that mean that it's kind of just hanging around out there and difficult to pin down?

Dylan doesn't often use the wind as a symbol of creativity; more often it has a harsh or destructive side to it – wind the destroyer rather than the pre-server, to use Shelley's two opposites from "Ode to the West Wind":

Wild Spirit, which are moving everywhere-
Destroyer and Preserver-hear, O hear!

Dylan likes the image of the wind howling – there's the howlin' winds in "Girl from the North Country", the howlin' wind and the outrageous snow in "Isis", and the end of "All Along the Watchtower":

Outside in the distance a wildcat did growl,
Two riders were approaching, the wind began to howl.

As well as the end of "Love minus Zero/No Limit":

The wind howls like a hammer,

---

64   Dunlap, J. "Through the eyes of Tom Joad: patterns of American idealism, Bob Dylan, and the Folk Protest Movement." *Popular Music and Society,* 2006, 13.

The night blows cold and rainy,
My love she's like some raven
At my window with a broken wing.

Hammers don't howl just as nights don't blow, but rarely have there been better mixed metaphors. There's also the wind hitting the traveller hard, which will be covered in chapter 4. That Dylan uses the wind as a destructive rather than a creative force may have something to do with an ambivalence about writing. A last example, another of his songs with "wind" in the title:

Idiot wind, blowing every time you move your mouth,

Idiot wind, blowing every time you move your teeth,

Idiot wind, blowing through the buttons of our coats,
Blowing through the letters that we wrote.

If the wind is a force linked to the creation of poetry in the English Romantic poets, in Dylan it is much closer to a destructive force, an idiot wind that blows everytime someone moves their mouth.

I'm just like that bird

Name me a poet who hasn't used the bird as a symbol of their art and ..... Our identification between birds and art goes way back, perhaps to the origins of literature, and we have long been fascinated by birds – their flight, their migration powers, their song. For the blind ancient Greek prophet Tiresias, the language of birds was the means to understand prophecy and the will of the gods, for example in Sophocles' "Antigone". In her feminist history of storytelling "From the Beast to the Blonde", Marina Warner looks at the history of fairy tales, and in an extraordinarily wide ranging discussion from the Sibyl in her labyrinth of caves in Cumae, to the stories of Angela Carter, she touches on the relation of birds and storytelling. She writes about the origins of "Mother Goose" tales, and the relation between what men deemed women's idle chatter and the song of birds. "Contes de la cigogne" (Tales of the Stork) was an alternative to the French phrase for fairy tales in the seventeenth century. Fairy tales were attributed to storks and geese – the origins of the phrase "Old Mother Goose", and the origins as well of the idea that storks bring babies, as women, including mid-wives, in Warner's view, would often tell tales that subverted the patriarchal order during the laying-in before childbirth.[65]

Birds have been used in literature and song in so many ways that it would be impossible to capture all the varieties of use here. Fortunately Graeme Gibson has compiled a "Bedside Book of Birds" which gathers some of the exceptional writing about birds as birds, and birds as symbols:

---

65   Warner, M. (1995) *From the Beast to the Blonde. On Fairy Tales and their Tellers*. London: Vintage.

At its heightened moments, birdwatching can encourage a state of being close to rapture. It is an ecstasy that is said to accompany the writing of poetry; sometimes it comes when we're listening to music….

Somewhere along the way we identified ourselves with them, and came to associate birds with the realm of spirits, as opposed to that of bodies and their carnal appetites.

Perhaps for this reason, there's an abundance of intriguing material about birds, from all times and all cultures. Not only do they feature in creation myths, in sagas and parables, in liturgies and in fairy tales, but poets, writers, story-tellers and artists in all ages have found them a fertile source of imagery and symbol.[66]

Gibson quotes the bibliophile Alberto Manguel, a writer who explores the history of writing on birds:

Outside my window is a cardinal. There is no way of writing this sentence without dragging in its tow whole libraries of literary allusions. The frame of the window and the margins of the page entrap the bird that serves as a sign for any bird, just as any bird serves as a sign for any idea. Noah's dove, Macbeth's rooks, Horace's swans, Omar Khayyam's pigeons, Theocritus'

---

66   Gibson, G. (2006) *The Bedside Book of Birds. An Avian Miscellany.* Anchor Canada, p. xii.

nightingale, Count Fosco's canaries – they are no longer birds, but usages of birds, feathered with words and meaning.[67]

Then there are the famous literary birds – Keats' nightingale, Yeats' golden bird of Byzantium, and Wallace Stevens' blackbird. For the English Romantics, the bird, like the wind, is often a symbol of song or of the spirit, as in Shelley's "To a Skylark":

Like a poet hidden
In the light of thought,
Singing hymns unbidden,
Till the world is wrought....

Or in Wordsworth's "The Solitary Reaper".

No Nightingale did ever chaunt
More welcome notes to weary bands
Of travellers in some shady haunt,
Among Arabian sands:

Wallace Stevens was a poet concerned with reading, writing, communication and the meaning or meaninglessness of symbols or words. Every second poem of his contains a reference to a bird, often in association with writing, as in "Thirteen Ways of Looking at a Blackbird":

Icicles filled the long window
With barbaric glass

---

67   Gibson, p. 17.

The shadow of the blackbird
Crossed it, to and fro.

Later in this book I write about one of Stevens' birds in "Of Mere Being", and also about ice, windows, wind and birds.

Add to the list of writers about birds one Bob Dylan. Dylan is knowledgeable about the uses of birds in folk songs, for example "Love Henry" which he recorded in 1993 on "World Gone Wrong" with a pretty acoustic backing, and which according to Gray dates back to at least 1827 as a Scottish folk ballad probably transferred to the Appalachians. The woman who kills her beloved Henry, who is about to leave her, appeals to a bird in the same way she has to Henry:

Fly down fly down pretty parrot she cried
And light on my right knee
The doors to your cage shall be decked with gold
And hung on a willow tree

I won't fly down and I can't fly down
And light on your right knee
A girl who would murder her own true love
Would kill a little bird like me.

What does the history of writing about birds tell us about these lines – which I keep coming back to - from "Love Minus Zero/No Limit "?:

The bridge at midnight trembles,
The country doctor rambles,

Bankers' nieces seek perfection,
Expecting all the gifts that wise men bring.
The wind howls like a hammer,
The night blows cold and rainy,
My love she's like some raven
At my window with a broken wing.

"My love she's like some raven" – the raven is at best an ambiguous bird and not one normally compared to a lover. First, we have Poe's raven, also discussed later in this book, and which Dylan knew, the "ungainly fowl" returning through the window to destroy the lover with the memory of love. Cawing ravens and crows are hardly sweet birds; Gibson quotes an eighteenth century passage about the raven[68]:

This bird has always been famous; but its bad reputation has been owing, most probably, to its being confounded with other birds, and loaded with their ill qualities. It has even been regarded most disgusting. Filth and rotten carcasses, it is said are its chief food.

Gibson also quotes from Audubon's writing on the raven in the Bible, where Noah during the flood first sends a raven to seek land:

Then Noah must have remembered that raven is an eater of carrion and would have found plenty of such fare exposed by the falling

68   Gibson, pp. 20 and 43.

waters….down through the ages the raven has had to bear the blame, becoming the symbol of ill omen and even death, the companion of witches and wizards and the embodiment of lost souls.

In the First Nations territory where I sit and write this book, the raven is both trickster and creator of humans. Ted Hughes follows this tradition in his book of poems, "Crow". Dylan may have been attracted to the alliterative association between "love" and "raven" and "rainy" in this most alliterative of stanzas; but we are also reminded of the dubious qualities of the raven by the double simile in the last four lines – "The wind howls like a hammer", "My love she's like some raven". As we saw in Chapter 2, this song is ambivalent at best about the loved one, as is the case in many of Dylan's so-called love songs, and the image of the raven fits in well.

What of Dylan's other uses of birds? Here are some other lines I keep coming back to:

Bird on the horizon, sittin' on a fence,
He's singin' his song for me at his own expense.
And I'm just like that bird, oh, oh,
Singin' just for you.
I hope that you can hear,
Hear me singin' through these tears.

What a painful, passionate song "You're a Big Girl Now" is. Dylan chooses the image of the bird here to express his pain, the pain of lost love and the pain of singing. But it's not the first bird on "Blood on the Tracks" – in fact Dylan is quite liberal with his use of birds on this album about the pain of love and singing. First in "Tangled up in Blue" the anonymous bird:

> *And when finally the bottom fell out*
> *I became withdrawn,*
> *The only thing I knew how to do*
> *Was to keep on keepin' on like a bird that flew,*
> *Tangled up in blue.*

Keeping on keeping on is at best an ambivalent response to becoming withdrawn, and the bird that's flying in this song might be equally out of control, with the suggestion of "flying the coop". In the next song, "Simple Twist of Fate", what seems like a throwaway reference:

> *He hears the ticking of the clocks*
> *And walks along with a parrot that talks,*
> *Hunts her down by the waterfront docks where*
> *the sailors all come in.*

Was Dylan just attracted to the alliteration here - "Ticking", "Clocks", "walks", "talks", "docks" – "docks" reminding us of the tick-tocking of clocks? Or is the parrot a reminder of the repetitions that are forced on an obsessed lover ("Blood on the Tracks" being among other things an album about different kinds of obsessive love), because the parrot is a bird that echoes what it hears. The parrot, a tropical bird, may also remind us of the hunting at the docks, and that parrots apparently become associated with pirates in the early 1700s when seamen traveling in the tropics would return home with the birds as souvenirs.

A couple of songs later were back at a softer comparison between bird and singer, on "Meet me in the Morning":

> *Little rooster crowin', there must be something on his mind*
> *Little rooster crowin', there must be something on his mind*
> *Well, I feel just like that rooster*
> *Honey, ya treat me so unkind.*

There's one more reference on "Blood on the Tracks", part of the code Dylan talked about when referring to this album, on "Shelter from the Storm":

> *I've heard newborn babies wailin' like a mournin' dove*
> *And old men with broken teeth stranded without love.*

References to mourning doves frequently appear in North American literature, as it is one of the most common species here; for example Robert Bly's "The Greek Ships", which also makes that connection between a bird, writing and pain: "I've heard that the mourning dove never says/What she means. / Those of us who make up poems/Have agreed not to say what the pain is." The wailing of the babies and bird song take us back to the other similes on the album – like the bird that flew, just like that bird, just like that rooster - all ancient literary symbol to which we instinctively respond.

There are no further references to birds on "Blood on the Tracks, but there is on one of the outtakes from that album, "Up to Me", a song that repeats many of the images from the album – singing, time, money and lost love:

Everything went from bad to worse, money never changed a thing,
Death kept followin', trackin' us down, at least I heard your bluebird sing.
Now somebody's got to show their hand, time is an enemy,
I know you're long gone,
I guess it must be up to me.

Clearly Dylan was pondering the processes of writing and singing, and their relation to lost love, through the image of the bird, one of the many "codes" which ties the album together, like the books discussed earlier in this chapter, and the road we will cover in chapter 4. What else has Dylan done with this most persistent of poetic images?

Dylan of course had used the image of the dove earlier in his work, in "Blowin' in the Wind":

Yes, 'n' how many seas must a white dove sail
Before she sleeps in the sand?

This is a much better known reference – to the dove that Noah sends out from the Ark in the Bible, and the dove which became a symbol of peace. When we see the reference to the white dove, super-charged with imagery over more than 2,000 years, we instantly get it, and listeners in the early 1960s, when the fear of nuclear war was everywhere in America and the peace movement was taking off, would have got it even quicker.

The white dove is also a common poetic denomi-nator, as I've suggested above with reference to "Shelter from the Storm". As well as representing peace, in early religions, doves were revered as the sacred companions of the gods. Early cultures including the Assyrians and Persians used white doves as a sacrificial bird, believing that the smoke rising from these burnt offerings would please the gods. The first archaeological evidence depicting doves as a spiritual bird dates back to 5000 BC, with the Sumerian goddess, Astarte. In the Bible, refer-ences to doves are always referential, and the Holy Spirit is often compared to a dove. In this sense the spiritual journey of the "man" in the first line of the "Blowin' in the Wind" is the same as that of the dove:

> How many roads must a man walk down
> Before you call him a man?
> Yes, 'n' how many seas must a white dove sail
> Before she sleeps in the sand?

In a song on the same album as "Blowin' in the Wind", "Don't Think Twice It's All Right", Dylan uses another bird to mark the passing of a relationship. "Don't Think

Twice" is partly a song about the difficulties of communicating, as I mentioned earlier in this chapter:

It ain't no use to sit and wonder why, babe
It don't matter, anyhow
An' it ain't no use to sit and wonder why, babe
If you don't know by now
When your rooster crows at the break of dawn
Look out your window and I'll be gone
You're the reason I'm trav'lin' on
Don't think twice, it's all right

Clearly the singer likes the idea of someone else looking out the window after him (if he's gone, why bother to look out the window?). But why the reference to the rooster, apart from the idea that he's leaving, romantically, before dawn, to head down the road. Like the dove, the rooster or cock has symbolic meaning. In the Talmud, the cock is seen as an indicator of the short moment in the day where God could be angry and would permit the cursing of a person by another (and there's certainly a bit of cursing in the song). In the Bible, the rooster provides the music for Christ's passion:

And Jesus said to him, "Truly I say to you, that this very night, before a rooster crows twice, you yourself will deny Me three times." (Mark 14: 30)

Wallace Stevens' use of the bird image in "The Man with the Blue Guitar", a poem like many of Stevens' about the act of creation and the gap between art and life, again using a bird image, is not incidental:

How long and late the pheasant sleeps…
The employer and employee contend,

…Spring sparkle and the cock-bird shriek.
The employer and employee will hear

And continue their affair. The shriek
Will rack the thickets. There is no place,

Here, for the lark fixed in the mind,
In the museum of the sky. The cock

Will claw sleep….

Note in "Don't Think Twice" it's the lover and not the singer that is compared to the bird:

When your rooster crows at the break of dawn
Look out your window and I'll be gone

He could have as easily sung "when that rooster", so the possessive here again suggests betrayal. Blind Willie McTell in "Love Changing Blues", recorded in 1929, made a similar comparison between the rooster and a perfidious women:

What do you want with a woman: when she
won't do nothing she say
What do you want with a rooster: when he won't
crow 'fore day
…. My woman done left me: I got these love-
changing blues

Weathercocks or roosters have adorned church steeples for centuries, a reminder of Christ's passion, and possibly to ward off evil. King Lear exclaims during the storm scene in Shakespeare's play:

Blow, winds, and crack your cheeks! rage! blow!
You cataracts and hurricanoes, spout
Till you have drench'd our steeples, drown'd the
cocks!

Dylan used Biblical imagery extensively in his early work, and throughout the album on which "Don't Think Twice" song appeared in 1962, "The Freewheelin' Bob Dylan". Dylan returns to a similar religious imagery in 1985 in "Dark Eyes" on "Empire Burlesque":

A cock is crowing far away and another soldier's
deep in prayer,
Some mother's child has gone astray, she can't
find him anywhere.
But I can hear another drum beating for the
dead that rise,
Whom nature's beast fears as they come and all
I see are dark eyes.

Talking of Blind Willie McTell, there's another bird reference, linking singer and bird, in Dylan's song of that name, written in 1983, but unreleased until the first three volumes of the Bootleg Series, in 1991:

Well, I heard that hoot owl singing
As they were taking down the tents

The stars above the barren trees
Was his only audience

No surprise to find a bird image in a song about a singer, but do owls really sing? And why choose the image of an owl in a song about a Blues singer? The owl is another ambiguous bird, bringer of doom and death, but also a wise bird, connected as a meditative bird to Minerva. Is that the dual image Dylan was trying to get across?

Enough of birds, words, letters and the fear of writing, time to move on down …the highway.

CHAPTER 4

Dylan's highway

Few symbols are closer to American hearts and desires than the highway. Without the highway, those lines crisscrossing the continent, there would be no modern cities, no suburbs, and no American dream. Travelling is a poetic common denominator which draws its power as an image from the way we have imbibed from an early age its uses in stories, songs and poems. Which is why the highway is so important to the songs of an American writer like Dylan.

The road is a potent myth in American literature, from Whitman's "Song of the Road", to Kerouac's "On the Road", to Guthrie's "Bound for Glory", to thousands of folk and blues songs. It's the most common theme in Dylan's songs, so to understand Dylan we need to understand how he uses the myth, the musical and literary traditions on which he draws for inspiration, and how he has taken that symbol onto new…paths. The idea of freedom has been associated with America, and many American writers have dealt with this theme and its opposite.

As Robert Butler writes: "A central quest in American life is for pure motion, movement either for its own sake or as a means of freeing oneself from a prior mode of existence...America has always set an unusually high premium on mobility. It is not surprising, therefore, that American literature is densely populated with .... fundamentally restless people in search of settings which are fluid enough to accommodate their passion for radical forms of freedom and independence. Cooper's West, Melville's ocean, Whitman's open road, and Twain's river are the mythic spaces that our classic heroes yearn for."[69] Steinbeck wrote about Americans in his road story "Travels with Charlie":

> I saw in their eyes something I was to see over and over in every part of the nation – a burning desire to go, to move, to get under way, anyplace, away from any here. They spoke quietly of how they wanted to go someday, to move about, free and unanchored, not toward something but away from something. I saw this look and heard this yearning everywhere in every state I visited.[70]

Pete Hamill wrote this about "Buckets of Rain" in the liner notes to the 1975 album "Blood on the Tracks":

---

69   (1998) *Contemporary African American Fiction: The Open Journey.* Madison: Farleigh Dickinson UP.
70   Steinbeck, J. (1962) *"Travels with Charley: In Search of America".* Penguin.

But a song which conjures up the American road, all the busted dreams of open places, boxcars, the Big Dipper pricking the velvet night. And it made me think of Ginsberg and Corso and Ferlinghetti, and most of all, Kerouac, racing Dean Moriarty across the country in the Fifties, embracing wind and night, passing Huck Finn on the riverbanks, bouncing against the Coast, and heading back again, with Kerouac dreaming his songs of the railroad earth.

The importance of the highway in Dylan's work has been recognized by several writers. As Louis Masur wrote:

By linking Dylan to Ellison, Melville, and Ginsberg, among many others, [Greil] Marcus reminds us that Dylan's work must be seen as part of a larger project to grapple with the tensions and ambiguities in American culture. Key to that enterprise is exploring the dream of escape that is at the center of the American experience. "Unmapped country," Marcus calls the contours of "Like a Rolling Stone," "hanging in the air as a territory of danger and flight, abandonment and discovery, truth and lie"...[71]

But the way in which Dylan explores and expands the highway theme, how roads become lines, lines become different kinds of boundaries, how

71   "Famous long ago. Bob Dylan revisited." *American Quarterly* 2007 vol. 59 (1), p. 176.

boundaries trap the traveler, and the tension between movement and being still has never been analysed in depth, and our understanding of Dylan's powerful lyrics is the lesser for this. It's also an image that binds his writing, from the early vagabond traveler, to the outsider, to the religious seeker on the ultimate road trip – trying to get to heaven before they close the door. And we'll take a look as well at who "they" are who want to close the door to keep the traveler out. Let's start with a review of the road in American literature, and then pick up on Dylan's brilliant adaptation of this, and look at: how he uses the image of the hard road; the wandering outsider; the link between wandering and wondering and hard thinking on the road; the road as boundary; and other boundaries and traps which the writer has such difficulty going beyond in his quest to be still and moving – such as doors and windows.

American culture has many uses for the road, the highway and train tracks. American movies and literature obsess about exploring that "dream of escape that is at the center of American experience." There is the road which ends nowhere – think the movie "Thelma and Louise", where the two road characters disappear into space, or Huck Finn, which ends: "But I reckon I got to light out for the Territory ahead of the rest, because Aunt Sally she's going to adopt me and sivilize me, and I can't stand it. I been there before." At the end of the great American novel, the main character vanishes at the end of the road. In "On the Road" Dean Moriarty disappears across America again on the book's last page. In

Steinbeck's the "Grapes of Wrath", another road story where the Joad family travel from Oklahoma to California, we lose sight of the hero Tom Joad towards the end of the book.

Bruce Springsteen's album "The Ghost of Tom Joad", a '90s remake of "The Grapes of Wrath", depicts the '90s Okies who have lost their place in American society. Like Steinbeck, Springsteen writes about people who have nowhere to go. The title song starts:

Men walkin' 'long the railroad tracks
Goin' someplace there's no goin' back

That grim picture of men on the railroad tracks – not even on a train for them to ride on - is complemented by the "goin' someplace", or nowhere to go. The rhyme on "back" takes us back to the railroad tracks, suggesting the railroad tracks aren't going anywhere either. At the end of another song on "The Ghost of Tom Joad", "Highway 29", the central character goes the way of many an American hero or anti-hero and disappears:

The road was filled with broken glass and gasoline
She wasn't sayin' nothin'', it was just a dream….
I closed my eyes and I was runnin',
I was runnin' then I was flyin'

Going into the unknown is common in Dylan's lyrics - "I'm heading down that long lonesome road babe, where I'm bound, I can't tell." from "Don't Think Twice It's Alright". We'll come back to that track.

As Primeau put it in his study of literature of the road[72]:

> Americans are in love with roads and cars, and we celebrate this romance in song, poetry, film and video...the genre thrives in a culture where writers and readers share clearly articulated literary techniques to question, reaffirm, and explore who they are and where they are going.... For most of this century, Americans have treated the highway as sacred space. Roads and cars have long gone beyond simple transportation to become places of exhilarating motion, speed, and solitude. Getting away is a chance at a new start, special time to discover self and country, glide through vast empty spaces and then come home to write or sing about the adventures. In hundreds of books, movies, poems, songs and videos, the road journey is an epic quest, a pilgrimage, a romance, a ritual that helps explain where Americans have been and where they think they might be going. Accordingly, the art forms and cultural symbols that have developed express a mode of consciousness, a complex of values, a way of seeing the world. Since the 1950s readers have been fascinated by who goes on the road as well as why, when, and where they go and what they discover along the way.

Dylan picked up on road images from multiple sources, but perhaps originally from English ballads

---

72   Primeau, Ronald (1996) *Romance of the Road*. Bowling Green: Bowling Green State University Popular Press, pp. ix-x, 1.

and Blues songs.[73] The road is so common in Dylan that there's scarcely a song that doesn't refer to the highway ("Down the highway, down the tracks, down the road to ecstasy"), the avenue ("We'll meet again on the avenue"), crossroads ("From the cross-roads of my doorstep"), the (railway) tracks, traveling or walking down the line ("I'm living in a foreign country, but I'm bound to cross the line'"), the path ("Though I'm travelin' on a path beaten trail"), the train ("Some trains don't pull no gamblers", maybe because the highway is for gamblers[74]), the street, (nobody ever taught you how to live out on it), cars ("We drove that car as far as we could"), as well as other images of travelling ("I'm sailing away my own true love" and a "piece of an old ship that lies by the shore"), and maps ("you gimme a map and a key to your door"). As Scobie has written: "Images of travel are everywhere in Dylan's songs, which are populated by roving gamblers, by young men on a train going west, by older men who have 'been all around the world,' by unknown riders approaching, and by singers bidding a 'restless farewell'."[75]

Here's an example from one Dylan album to make the point, but I could have chosen any of his records. On "Time out of Mind" the first song "Love Sick" starts:

---

73   For Dylan's extensive debts to these sources, see Gray, chapter 9, and on the highway pp. 293-6. Dylan was also influenced by songs such as "Wandering" sung among others by Josh White Senior - thanks to Gerry Beck for that last reference.

74   Or because Woody Guthrie sang "This train is bound for glory".

75   Scobie, p. 32.

I'm walking through streets that are dead
Walking, walking with you in my head

The second song "Dirt Road Blues" speaks for itself. The third "Standing in the Doorway" starts:

I'm walking through the summer nights

And the first verse of the fifth song "Tryin' to Get to Heaven" goes:
The air is getting hotter
There's a rumbling in the skies
I've been wading through the high muddy water
With the heat rising in my eyes
Every day your memory grows dimmer
It doesn't haunt me like it did before
I've been walking through the middle of nowhere
Trying to get to heaven before they close the door

And so on. That "walking through the middle of nowhere" with a woman on his mind is SO Dylan. And where, exactly, is the "middle of nowhere"?

The first person traveler a long way from home is the most common Dylan road image. It's there from the first publicly released self-written song "Song to Woody":

I'm out here a thousand miles from my home,
Walkin' a road other men have gone down.

> *I'm a-leaving' tomorrow, but I could leave today,*
> *Somewhere down the road someday.*

"Somewhere down the road someday" – ah, so vague and romantic! But also a clever contrast between the present – today – the near future – tomorrow – and the far distant future – someday – a contrast Dylan uses again and again, and to which we return in the next chapter when looking at Dylan and time.

On his recent album "Modern Times" Dylan sings on "Ain't Talkin":

> *Ain't talking, just walking*
> *Up the road, around the bend.*
> *Heart burning, still yearning*
> *In the last outback at the world's end.*

The point about "around the bend" is, usually we don't know what's there. The world's end is both the mythical destination of sailors, the final end of the road, or the end of the world, in the biblical sense. And it's a repetition that would have done Christopher Ricks proud – not only the "world's end" but also the "last outback".[76] It's also the "middle of nowhere" from "Tryin' to get to heaven", the place where the walker disappears. In "Ain't Talking", released in 2006 and quoted second below, we hear too about the long and lonesome road of

---

[76]   On Dylan's use of cliché, see Ricks, Christopher (2004). "Excerpt from 'The Force of Poetry' " in Hedin, Benjamin (ed). *Studio A. The Bob Dylan Reader*. New York: W.W. Norton pp. 137-46.

"Don't Think Twice, It's Allright" (quoted first below), released 33 years earlier:

I'm walkin' down that long lonesome road babe.

Ain't no altars on this long and lonesome road

That long lonesome road which stretches across Dylan's recording career stretches back as well to the numerous variations of "Lonesome Road Blues", such as the one sung by Fields Ward and recorded by Alan Lomax in 1937:

Oh, look up and down that long, lonesome road,
Hang down your head and cry, my love,
Hang down your head and cry.
Oh, I wish to the Lord I had never been born,
Or died when I was a baby, my love,
Or died when I was a baby…..
You caused me to weep, you caused me to mourn,
You caused me to leave my home, my love,
You caused me to leave my home.[77]

Ramblin' Jack Elliott's version of "Lonesome Road Blues" contains the line "I'm going down the road feeling bad", which Dylan uses as "I'm just going down the road feeling bad" in "Tryin' to Get to Heaven", a line which seems out of place until you realize its heritage as a common line in the traveling

---

77   See http://www.ibiblio.org/keefer/index.htm See also Gene Austen's version of "Lonesome Road".

blues. Blame and travel are also central to "Don't Think Twice, it's Allright", as they are to Fields Ward's and Gene Austen's songs. In "Don't Think Twice, it's Allright" another women has caused the singer's departure, and it's among the first of many accusatory songs in Dylan's repertoire – forget love and hate, blame is surely the greatest human emotion:

When your rooster crows at the break of dawn
Look out your window and I'll be gone
You're the reason I'm trav'lin' on

Being a long way from home is also a favorite theme. Here are a few examples:: "A thousand miles from home" ("I Believe in You"); "The only place open is a thousand miles away and I can't take you there" ("Don't Fall Apart on Me Tonight"); and "'One too many mornings and a thousand miles behind."[78]

Dylan borrowed this image from the Guthriesque troubadour who travels far from home with guitar in hand from camp fire to camp fire, the quintessential outsider. Dylan raved about Guthrie's lonely planet guide to the underside of America, "Bound for Glory" in the late 1950s.[79] As many have written, in his early songs, such as "Song to Woody",

---

78   Jimmie Rogers traveling song "Waitin' for a train" ends: "I'm a thousand miles away from home/Just waitin' for a train."
79   Dylan, Bob (2004) *Chronicles. Volume 1*. New York: Simon and Schuster. Dylan's annotated copy of "Bound for Glory" was discovered recently in a closet in a bedroom he had stayed in in Greenwich village in the early 1960s - a remarkable piece of musical archaelogy if ever there was one.

and early interviews, Dylan invented a romantic hard-bitten figure coming to New York. This follows another American cultural road tradition, the unsophisticated traveler coming from the country to the supposedly sophisticated city, only to expose its superficiality and dens of iniquity – think Superman, Crocodile Dundee, Eddie Murphy and King Kong coming in from out of town to New York, or Lydia Bennett coming to London from the country with Wickham in "Pride and Prejudice". Dylan has his own version in the early "Talking New York":

> Ramblin' outa the wild West,
> Leavin' the towns I love the best.
> Thought I'd seen some ups and down,
> "Til I come into New York town.
> People goin' down to the ground,
> Buildings goin' up to the sky…
>
> I walked down there and ended up
> In one of them coffee-houses on the block.
> Got on the stage to sing and play,
> Man there said, "Come back some other day,
> You sound like a hillbilly;
> We want folk singers here."

He revisits the same theme forty or so years later on "Mississippi":

> City's just a jungle, more games to play
> Trapped in the heart of it, trying to get away
> I was raised in the country, I been workin' in the town

I been in trouble ever since I set my suitcase down

And with an equal sense of restlessness he is keen to get back to the city in "Watching the River Flow":

Wish I was back in the city
Instead of this old bank of sand,
With the sun beating down over the chimney tops
And the one I love so close at hand.

There is a reverse tradition of course, also epitomized in King Kong, with the supposedly sophisticated city slicker heading, usually reluctantly, to the country, only to find that under its bumpkin exterior there is a sense of community long-lost in the metropolis – think Harrison Ford in "Witness" heading to the idealized Mennonite community (with its house raising scenes so beloved of Hollywood script writers, a kind of rural community pimp my house), or Michael J. Fox, the work obsessed L.A. doctor finding true love in "Doc Hollywood" where the mayor and other town folk dress up as... vegetables (you don't get much more hillbilly than that). Or the city slicker who has to learn how to make out in the hostile country – romantic novelist Joan Wilder traveling to the jungles of Colombia in "Romancing the Stone", or the feature writer from "Newsday" heading for the Australian outback in "Crocodile Dundee" - the movie which plays it both ways. And so at the end of "Talking New York" the so-called hillbilly heads back to the hills:

So one mornin' when the sun was warm,
I rambled out of New York town.
Pulled my cap down over my eyes
And headed out for the western skies.
So long, New York.
Howdy, East Orange.

As Carole Childs said about Dylan's travels: "This is his trade. This is the troubadour in him. This is what troubadours did. This is what vaudevillians did. This is what burlesque people did. This is what you do. You entertain people."[80] There's a much longer literary tradition than that of Guthrie, as this quote suggests. Troubadours wrote in southern France during medieval times, but their songs were influenced by earlier traditions such as Arabic poetry from 10 centuries earlier. The universal themes of Troubadour songs – love, singing, traveling, searching - were picked up by ballad writers in medieval Europe, the English Romantic poets at the beginning of the nineteenth century, from whom there is a direct link to Waltman and Guthrie, and to Dylan.[81]

The wandering outsider

Dylan's characterization of the traveler is common in romantic poetry. The U.S. 1930s and '40s writers

---

80   Quoted in Sounes, Howard (2001) *Down the Highway*, Grove Press, p. 441. Sounes' biography itself ends with Dylan drifting "way out into the heart of America and on around the world." (ibid).
81   See Gray; and Carman, Bryan. *A Race of Singers. Whitman's Working-Class Hero from Guthrie to Springsteen*. University of North Carolina Press, 2000.

and singers about the road drew on earlier English romantic traditions. Poets such as Wordsworth were observing a social transformation similar to that during the American dust bowl. As the industrial revolution progressed in early 19th century England, usually exploitative social bonds which kept villagers tied to their villages broke down, and there were a greater number of poor homeless people on the road, looking for work, and migrating to cities.[82] Dylan's travelers look back to those of the English romantic poets in a very particular way – the idea of the traveler on the road, cold, hungry and poor, but also the idea of the traveler as outside of society, someone who by being on the road is a "stranger" and has broken social norms. Dylan's earlier songs in particular make references to carnivals, joints, fairgrounds, hobos, vagabonds, tramps, bandits, pirates, as did Guthrie before Dylan with his attention to the hobo. Springsteen does the same on "The Ghost of Tom Joad", an album about ordinary people doing extraordinary things.

The outlaw has always been a popular literary character, and one with whom artists – often outsiders themselves - have long associated. The poet, by his or her sensibilities, is also on the margins of society, or out of bounds – which is why boundaries are important in Dylan's writing.

---

82   Thompson, E.P (1963) *The Making of the English Working Class*. London: Penguin.

Primeau writes[83]:

> From picaresque tales, the road story gives us ras-
> cals and rogues who wander aimlessly to under-
> mine the status quo in episodic adventures that
> mock acceptable routines and values. Like the
> picaro antihero, protagonists on the road are cut
> loose from everyday restraints and of work and
> daily experiences. As they revel in their wander-
> ing, picaro road characters may have difficulty
> with, or even refuse, reintegration and choose
> instead to extend their journey indefinitely.

"Wander" is a good word to describe the way Dylan
writes about travel. It means to "move about without a fixed course" or to go idly about, like many
of the characters in Dylan's songs. But while those
characters wander, they usually have something on
their mind. Let's look at Dylan's use of wandering
and wondering.

Wordsworth's "The Daffodils" is an early variant
about the wandering creator. It starts:

> I wandered lonely as a Cloud
> That floats on high o'er Vales and Hills,
> When all at once I saw a crowd,
> A host of golden daffodils;

---

83   ibid, p. 7

And ends:

> *For oft when on my couch I lie* .
> *In vacant or in pensive mood*

Dylan's 1974/5 song "Tangled up in Blue", from "Blood on the Tracks", neatly reverses Wordsworth's order, starting with emotion recollected in turbulence, the narrator in pensive mood on his couch:

> *Early one mornin' the sun was shinin',*
> *I was layin' in bed*
> *Wond'rin' if she'd changed at all*

And ending with wandering:

> *But me, I'm still on the road*
> *Headin' for another joint*

That tension between being still and wondering on one hand, and being on the road and wandering on the other, is a key one in Dylan just as it was in earlier Romantic poets.[84] It's a theme I'll come back

---

84   For Wordsworth "couch" meant a place to sleep or bed. Ricks (2005) notes (p. 115): "But Dylan, as an heir of Romanticism (Blake's and Keats's, for a start), was sure to be drawn to imagine in depth those slothful-looking moods or modes that smilingly put it to us that we might put in a good word for them. Sloth is bad, but "wise passiveness" (Wordsworth) is the condition of many a good thing, including the contemplative arts in both their creation and reception." Coleridge was apparently no slouch and could walk the 25 miles between his and the Wordsworths' cottage in a few hours. But sick one time for three months he lay in bed, examining light as it passed through a glass prism. See Holmes, R. (1990) *Coleridge. Early Visions.* Viking Press. Whitman's wandering is full of wondering, as is Van Morrison's in "Sense of Wonder".

to later in this chapter and what is, fittingly, the last chapter of this book, on time.

Dylan pulls off a sweet pun in his 1963 song "Don't Think Twice, It's Alright" – "I'm a-thinkin' and a-wond'rin'" all the way down the road". Is he wandering or wondering – Dylan's wanderers do both? The song starts:

It ain't no use to sit and wonder why, babe.

She isn't allowed to wonder, but he can wonder all the way down the road, while the narrator in "Tangled up in Blue" can not only sit, but lie and wonder:

Early one mornin' the sun was shinin',
I was layin' in bed
Wond'rin' if she'd changed at all

The English ballad "Early One Morning", another song about blame and lost love, and discussed later in this chapter in relation to "Tangled up in Blue", includes the verse:

Here I now wander alone as I wonder
Why did you leave me to sigh and complain?
I ask of the roses, why should I be forsaken?
Why must I here in sorrow remain?

The Christmas song "I wonder as I wander", was collected by John Jacob Niles in the 1930s in the Appalachian Mountains.

Henry Miller made a similar link in his musings about his trip to discover America: "It is only the wonderful traveler who sees a wonder."[85]

Wandering, or moving about without a fixed course or going idly about defies social norms, which is what the outsider or traveler or stranger does. Outside of normal bounds, not following the rules, travelers and strangers are threatening. In Wordsworth's "The Leech-Gatherer", the leech gatherer's continual wandering troubles the poet:

While he was talking thus, the lonely place,
The Old-man's shape, and speech, all troubled me:
In my mind's eye I seemed to see him pace
About the weary moors continually,
Wandering about alone and silently.

In Blake's fragment: "Never Seek to Tell thy Love", a poem I analyse throughout this book, the outsider is the traveler who steals love:

Never seek to tell thy love
Love that never told can be;
For the gentle wind does move
Silently, invisibly.

I told my love, I told my love,
I told her all my heart,

---

85   From Henry Miller's 1945 'The Air-Conditioned Nightmare', quoted in Primeau, p. 36.

Trembling, cold, in ghastly fears–
Ah, she doth depart.

Soon as she was gone from me
A traveller came by
Silently, invisibly–
He took her with a sigh.

Dylan's also uses such outsiders, like the one in the long black coat:

Somebody seen him hanging around
At the old dance hall on the outskirts of town,
He looked into her eyes when she stopped to ask
If he wanted to dance, he had a face like a mask.

Off she goes with that traveler, and off she goes silently –

Not a word of goodbye, note even a note,
She gone with the man
In the long black coat.

Note he has been hanging around on the outskirts of town – and having a face like a mask can never be a good sign.

In each verse of "Like a Rolling Stone" – a song about an insider who has become an outsider – there's a different kind of stranger– the bum who gets the dime, the jugglers and the clowns, the mystery tramp, and Napoleon in rags – just to make the point that the rolling stone is now on a par with these folk. The album "Highway 61 Revisited" is packed with outsiders – the sword swallower, the one eyed midget in "Ballad of a Thin Man", the clowns – again – and bandits in "Queen Jane Approximately", the rovin' gambler in "Highway 61 Revisited", and the multiple characters in "Desolation Row". But in "Desolation Row" Dylan reverses the tradition. If Springsteen's songs are about ordinary people doing extraordinary things as outsiders, "Desolation Row" is about extraordinary people doing ordinary things – sweeping up, playing electric violin, reciting the alphabet. No longer threatening, these outsiders have become banal.

Like the woman in "Like a Rolling Stone", there's another kind of outsider in Dylan's songs, the individual who is damaged by society or society's norms. This is why figures of authority in Dylan's songs – that is people who define and maintain social norms - are almost always figures of disdain or fun, and why outcasts are so popular. His "protest" songs often focus on the individual, which is part of the reason they are so effective – "Seven Curses", "The Lonesome Death of Hattie Carroll", "The Death of Emmett Till", "Only a Pawn in Their Game", "Percy's Song", "Hurricane", and "Joey" all refer to individuals wrongly treated by the law or society and ill-judged. And Dylan writes of "Lenny Bruce":

He was an outlaw, that's for sure,
More of an outlaw than you ever were

Lenny Bruce is dead but he didn't commit any crime

They said that he was sick 'cause he didn't play by the rules
He just showed the wise men of his day to be nothing more than fools.

In Dylan's songs the "law" is almost referred to with disdain, as are rules:

Although the masters make the rules
For the wise men and the fools

You got gangsters in power and lawbreakers making rules.

This links to Dylan's religious songs – people making rules just ain't a good idea. Dylan is well known for the individualistic approach of his songs, refusing to be labelled, to sign on to popular causes, to be considered a "protest" singer, or to do what was expected of him. As Dunlap comments: "One of the principal traits of Dylan's mature rhetorical songs was his implied challenge to received wisdom of all kinds."[86]

Me, I

If the traveler is the lone outsider on the road, the opposite of the traveler is society or other people.

---

86   James Dunlap "Through the eyes of Tom Joad: patterns of American idealism, Bob Dylan, and the Folk Protest Movement." *Popular Music and Society*, December 2006, p. 18.

Primeau writes: "road narratives might argue for the individual in a mass-dominated society by celebrating the residual values of the pioneers of the frontier."[87] Dylan picked up from the romantic poets the notion of the lone artist using their muse to battle against the world's injustice. As Shelley put is in "The Defense of Poetry": "Poets, according to the circumstances of the age and nation in which they appeared, were called, in the earlier epochs of the world, legislators, or prophets: a poet essentially comprises and unites both these characters." The artist is singled out by inspiration (originally meaning "a divine influence or action on a person believed to qualify him or her to receive and communicate sacred revelation" or someone who received God's breath), as an outsider whose intense personal experiences reveal truth.

In Dylan most often this reveals itself in the phrasing "me, I", which is contrasted to "people" or "they" – so much so that this opposition of the outsider to "people" is another organizing feature of his songs. Here are a few examples:

> Grandpa died last week
> And now he's buried in the rocks,
> But everybody still talks about
> How badly they were shocked.
> But me, I expected it to happen,
>
> Everybody's wearing a disguise
> To hide what they've got left behind their eyes

---

87   Primeau p. 4.

But me I can't cover what I am

All the people we used to know
They're an illusion to me now.
Some are mathematicians
Some are carpenter's wives.
Don't know how it all got started,
I don't know what they're doin' with their lives.
But me, I'm still on the road

What's the matter with me,
I don't have much to say....
People disagreeing on all just about everything,
yeah,
Makes you stop and all wonder why.

Don't let me change my heart,
Keep me set apart
From all the plans they do pursue.
And I, I don't mind the pain[88]

That contrast between "people" or "'crowd" and the singer or the "I'" in the song is a common theme in "Blood on the Tracks":

Later on when the crowd thinned out
I was just about to do the same

I seen a lot of women

---

88   "Stuck Inside of Mobile with the Memphis Blues Again"; "Abandoned Love"; "Tangled up in Blue"; "Watin' the River Flow"; "I Believe in You".

People see me all the time
And they just can't remember how to act

I see a lot of people
As I make the rounds

People tell me it's a sin
To know and feel too much within[89]

This last referring to the idea that knowing and feeling too much within is against social norms. Here are a few other references to make the point:

I'm gonna have to put up a barrier to keep myself away from everyone.

There's too many people, too many to recall
I thought some of 'm were friends of mine; I was wrong about 'm all

All these people that you mention
Yes I know them they're quite lame

I used to be among the crowd you're in with

I got my back to the sun 'cause the light is too intense
I can see what everybody in the world is up against[90]

---

89   "Tangled up in Blue"; "Idiot Wind"; "If You See Her, Say Hello"; "Simple Twist of Fate".
90   "Dirt Road Blues"; "Cold Irons Bound"; "Desolation Row"; "Positively 4th Street; "Sugar Baby".

The idea of me against them also reverberates through Dylan's religious songs:

Ring them bells for the chosen few

And You've chosen me to be among the few

My so-called friends have fallen under a spell[91]

There are many other references in Dylan's songs – chose your album, choose your song. But, as for me, my own personal favorite that I like best is from a song built around the contrast between the singer and everybody else – "I'll Keep it with Mine":

Ev'rybody will help you
Some people are very kind.
But if I can save you any time,
Come on, give it to me,
I'll keep it with mine.

We have in this song an early playing with words out of place, in this case the possessive pronoun "mine", although for the most part Dylan prefers playing with adjectives and adverbs, as we've seen in chapter 2 on "Blonde and Blonde" and love and sex.

---

91   "Ring Them Bells"; "What Can I Do for You"; "Precious Angel".

Faces in the crowd

If the artist separates him/herself out from other people, what's often left of the others is their faces. Here's another wanderer in Blake's "London":

> I wander thro each charter'd street,
> Near where the charter'd Thames does flow.
> And mark in every face I meet
> Marks of weakness, marks of woe.

What Blake does as he wanders through each street is both to separate the wanderer from "every face", but also through use of the term "mark in every face", to associate himself with the people he sees as he wanders, through his own "marking" of others. Similarly Dylan is always connected in some way to the faces that he meets.

The idea of "every face" in the crowd is another common literary theme, as in Ezra Pound's "In a Station of the Metro":

> The apparition of these faces in the crowd
> petals on a wet, black bough.

Pound wrote: "Three years ago in Paris I got out of a 'metro' train at La Concorde, and saw suddenly a beautiful face, and then another and another, and then a beautiful child's face, and then another beautiful woman, and I tried all that day to find words for what this had meant to me, and I could not find any words that seemed to me worthy, or as lovely as that sudden emotion."[92]

Contemporaries of Dylan cover similar ground, looking at the faces in the crowd, for example Springsteen on "Long Walk Home" from his 2007 album "Magic":

> In town I passed Sal's grocery
> The barbershop on South Street
> I looked into their faces
> They were all strangers to me

Dylan reverses this on "Mississippi" (from " 'Love and Theft' ", released in 2001):

> Walking through the leaves, falling from the trees
> Feeling like a stranger nobody sees

A similar theme is expressed in Springsteen's "Human Touch", where he writes about the lack of kindness in the face of strangers, and in Tom Petty's "A Face in the Crowd". The Be Good Tanyas echo Blake in "Song to R" singing about people coming from all sides with broken hearts and hollow eyes. And another Canadian heroine, Jane Siberry, wrote in similar fashion in "The Gospel According to Darkness" about looking around at the people on the street.

Face in Dylan is a complicated word, and one he uses a lot. There's the straightforward usage in

---

92   (1916) *Gaudier-Brzeska: A Memoir*, John Lane.

"Tangled up in Blue" – "I just kept lookin' at the side of her face". Then there's the formulation noted above, pointing to the difference between the narrator/singer and everyone else:

A million faces at my feet but all I see are dark eyes.

Shouldn't it be something like "the world at my feet" or "you should kneel at my feet"? But as Dylan said: "When I'm up there, I just see faces. A face is a face, they are all the same."[93] After going through the cast of characters in "Desolation Row", where Dylan has already rearranged their faces and given them all another name, he writes:

All these people that you mention
Yes, I know them, they're quite lame
I had to rearrange their faces
And give them all another name

Does he mean he has to put one face in place of another, or move the eyes and noses around, or both? And there are other lines which similarly uses others' faces to reiterate the "me" against "them" image:

They say ev'rything can be replaced,
Yet ev'ry distance is not near.
So I remember ev'ry face
Of ev'ry man who put me here....

---

93   Quoted in Ricks, *Dylan's Visions of Sin*, p. 490.

Standing next to me in this lonely crowd,
Is a man who swears he's not to blame.

I've said goodbye to haunted rooms and faces
in the street

The driver peeks out, trying to find one face
In this concrete world full of souls.

In the broken mirror of innocence on each for-
gotten face.[94]

And what a beautiful contrast – in "Most of the Time"
between the line:

I can smile in the face of mankind

And:

Don't even remember what her lips felt like on
mine

As Ricks points out: "there is no smile on the face of
the line that leads to those lips of hers and mine."[95]
The contrast between the face of mankind and her
lips brings us back to that "I" and "them", but also to
the fact that it's lips that smile.[96]

---

94   "I Shall be Released"; "Wedding Song"; "Three Angels"; "Every
Grain of Sand".
95   p. 355.
96   Like many English words, face has multiple meanings. Dylan
uses it without the contrast to others in his love songs, for example in
"Sad-Eyed Lady of the Lowlands".

To the lone singer on the road, everyone else becomes a stranger or a face.[97] That loneliness, the contrast with the undifferentiated crowd, ties to a key image in Dylan, the borderline, because it's the border that separates and excludes.

The hard road and the silent traveler

Whitman opens his "Song of the Road" as follows:

Afoot and light-hearted I take to the open road,
Healthy, free, the world before me,
The long brown path before me leading wherever I choose.

As opposed to Whitman's open road, there's nothing easy about being on the road Dylan writes about, it's usually cold, uncomfortable and maybe not leading anywhere. When Dylan writes about the road, whoever he is writing about is alone:

So if you're travelin' in the north country fair,
Where the winds hit heavy on the borderline,

One look at his face showed the hard road he'd come
And a fistful of coins showed the money he bummed.

Oh the weather is against me and the wind blows hard

---

97   For an analysis of self and identity in Dylan, see Scobie.

And the rain she's a-turnin' into hail.
I still might strike it lucky on a highway goin' west,
Though I'm travelin' on a path beaten trail.

An' it ain't no use in turnin' on your light, babe
I'm on the dark side of the road[98]

And I was standin' on the side of the road[99]
Rain fallin' on my shoes
Heading out for the East Coast
Lord knows I've paid some dues gettin' through

Despite this whining, the road has a romantic pull, and in Dylan's songs it's better to be on the road than stuck back home, again from "Tangled Up in Blue".

So now I'm goin' back again,
I got to get to her somehow.
All the people we used to know
They're an illusion to me now.
Some are mathematicians
Some are carpenter's wives.

---

98   "Girl from the North Country"; "Only a Hobo"; "Farewell"; "Don't Think Twice, It's All Right"; "Tangled Up In Blue". Which is the dark side of the road – is it the opposite side to the popular tune, the sunny side of the street?

99   Why is he standing on the side of the road? Waiting for a ride? Is it the dark side of the road? In the notebook in which Dylan wrote the original lyrics of "Blood on the Tracks", he wrote "And he was walking by the side of the road." Is it being caught between wanting to move on and stay? Does he want to draw attention to the other three references to 'side' on "Blood on the Tracks"'? What is that joint he's heading for, anyway – we'll consider that line later, and see the section on "Tangled up in Blue" later in this chapter?

Don't know how it all got started,
I don't know what they're doin' with their lives.
But me, I'm still on the road
Headin' for another joint

Better to be on the road than to be an illusion, a mathematician or a carpenter's wife, or to stay in one place – here's "Guess I'm doin' fine":

Well, my road might be rocky,
The stones might cut my face.
My road it might be rocky,
The stones might cut my face.
But as some folks ain't got no road at all,
They gotta stand in the same old place.
Hey, hey, so I guess I'm doin' fine.

This is why I agree with Ricks about "Like a Rolling Stone":[100]

How does it feel
To be without a home

Does the answer have to be terrible, terrifying? Is there nothing about being without a home that could be, even if far short of terrific, at least freed from certain pressures and oppressions? (Ask any artist whose life, by and large, is on the road). Or freed from certain sadnesses?

---

100   "Dylan's Vision of Sin", p. 182. Scobie in "Alias Bob Dylan Revisited" makes a similar point.

Primeau writes: "Kerouac is best understood when you are older, for after all the hitchhiking and mad-cap driving and zany adventures, his despair lingers…His final message is that you've got to get out and look for America-both within yourself and on the road- and no matter what you find, you are better off than sitting in a cage".[101]

Supporting this is Dylan's "Not Dark Yet":

> *I was born here and I'll die here against my will*
> *I know it looks like I'm moving, but I'm standing still*

"Standing still" is the exact opposite of being "still on the road" (from "Tangled up in Blue"), using the positioning of "still" to suggest both stasis and movement. Fortunately things get moving again on "Modern Times", walking if not talking. There's more on "stillness" in Dylan's songs and those of others, and the poems of other writers such as T.S. Eliot, in chapter 5.

Which brings us to what the romantic traveler does on the road. If the road is lonely, it is also a place of silence. In Wordsworth's "Resolution and Independence", already quoted, the old man who gathers leeches for a living is: "Wandering about alone and silently."

---

101   37-38, quoting Brinkley, Douglas. (1994) *The Magic Bus: An American Odyssey.* New York: Doubleday-Anchor, p. 22

Springsteen again on "Highway 29" makes the link between the road and silence:

> The road was filled with broken glass and gasoline
> The wind come silent through the windshield
> I closed my eyes and I was runnin',
> I was runnin' then I was flyin'

Or Blake's silent traveler in "Never seek to tell thy love":

> Soon as she was gone from me
> A traveller came by
> Silently, invisibly–
> He took her with a sign.

In Dylan the road is also often a place of silence:

> Ain't talkin', just walkin'

> I'm a-thinkin' and a-wond'rin' all the way down the road[102]

In two other songs Dylan contrasts the silence outside as he wanders. Here is "One Too Many Mornings":

> An' the silent night will shatter
> From the sounds inside my mind,
> For I'm one too many mornings
> And a thousand miles behind.

---

102   "Ain't Talkin'"; "Don't Think Twice it's All Right".

And here is "Love Sick":

I'm walking through streets that are dead
Walking, walking with you in my head

Sometimes the silence can be like the thunder
Sometimes I wanna take to the road and plunder
Could you ever be true?
I think of you
And I wonder

Here we have the silent traveler whose thoughts explode as he wanders and wonders. What better romantic image is there of the suffering artist? As Paul Williams has said, Dylan is the traveling performer who makes and remakes his art on a continual basis.[103] There's a kind of salvation and therapy in creating and performing which can't be found in other kinds of human activity. The point about wandering and wondering is that the hard road leads to the process which is central to creating. There's a connection between traveling, silence and creation. Primeau comments[104]: "In one way or another, every highway hero wants to get away from the distractions of everyday life and drive into a time and place where the inner self can emerge." But this perpetual motion itself becomes a kind of trap because the artist ends up "making the rounds" or

---

103   *Bob Dylan: Mind Out of Time (Performing Artist Vol. 3, 1987-2000)*. Omnibus Press. 2004.
104   1996, p.69.

being "still on the road", which we'll come to in a moment.

"Tangled up in Blue"

Travel song par excellence, on an album that is constantly on the move, "Tangled up in Blue", released in 1975, has also been the clarion call at Dylan's concerts for the crowd to rush towards the stage, and is one of the most written about of his songs. Ross asks: "Why, night after night, did "Tangled up in Blue" prove to be the song that brought the audience to life, as if Dylan had dived in and given everyone a hug?"[105] Why indeed? It follows in a long tradition of such songs and ballads accompanying the narrator through trials and quests to reach a physical and spiritual goal. Primeau writes: "The unfolding of highway adventures and the organizational frames for telling about them generally follow predictable patterns, In turn, both the conventional patterns themselves as well as successive modifications of those patterns make books understandable for readers who know what to expect. Literary conventions also enable authors to introduce variations into the established order."[106] "Tangled up in Blue" in form and content is a common poetic denominator that we understand on a visceral level because of its familiarity.

---

105   Alex Ross (2004) "The Wanderer" in B. Hedin (ed) *Studio A: The Bob Dylan Reader*, New York: Norton4, p. 306.
106   Primeau p. 9.

Here are the lyrics on the official Dylan website:

Early one mornin' the sun was shinin',
I was layin' in bed
Wond'rin' if she'd changed at all
If her hair was still red.
Her folks they said our lives together
Sure was gonna be rough
They never did like Mama's homemade dress
Papa's bankbook wasn't big enough.
And I was standin' on the side of the road
Rain fallin' on my shoes
Heading out for the East Coast
Lord knows I've paid some dues gettin' through,
Tangled up in blue.

She was married when we first met
Soon to be divorced
I helped her out of a jam, I guess,
But I used a little too much force.
We drove that car as far as we could
Abandoned it out West
Split up on a dark sad night
Both agreeing it was best.
She turned around to look at me
As I was walkin' away
I heard her say over my shoulder,
"We'll meet again someday on the avenue,"
Tangled up in blue.

I had a job in the great north woods
Working as a cook for a spell

But I never did like it all that much
And one day the ax just fell.
So I drifted down to New Orleans
Where I happened to be employed
Workin' for a while on a fishin' boat
Right outside of Delacroix.
But all the while I was alone
The past was close behind,
I seen a lot of women
But she never escaped my mind, and I just grew
Tangled up in blue.

She was workin' in a topless place
And I stopped in for a beer,
I just kept lookin' at the side of her face
In the spotlight so clear.
And later on as the crowd thinned out
I's just about to do the same,
She was standing there in back of my chair
Said to me, "Don't I know your name?"
I muttered somethin' underneath my breath,
She studied the lines on my face.
I must admit I felt a little uneasy
When she bent down to tie the laces of my shoe,
Tangled up in blue.

She lit a burner on the stove and offered me a pipe
"I thought you'd never say hello," she said
"You look like the silent type."
Then she opened up a book of poems
And handed it to me

Written by an Italian poet
From the thirteenth century.
And every one of them words rang true
And glowed like burnin' coal
Pourin' off of every page
Like it was written in my soul from me to you,
Tangled up in blue.

I lived with them on Montague Street
In a basement down the stairs,
There was music in the cafes at night
And revolution in the air.
Then he started into dealing with slaves
And something inside of him died.
She had to sell everything she owned
And froze up inside.
And when finally the bottom fell out
I became withdrawn,
The only thing I knew how to do
Was to keep on keepin' on like a bird that flew,
Tangled up in blue.

So now I'm goin' back again,
I got to get to her somehow.
All the people we used to know
They're an illusion to me now.
Some are mathematicians
Some are carpenter's wives.
Don't know how it all got started,
I don't know what they're doin' with their lives.
But me, I'm still on the road
Headin' for another joint
We always did feel the same,

We just saw it from a different point of view,
Tangled up in blue.

Dylan recorded an earlier widely circulated version of the song in 1974, with lyrics fairly similar to those above.[107] But the lyrics have changed as Dylan has sung the song in concert over the years, changing the person and in the *Real Live* version, released in 1984, changing several stanzas. The phrase "carpenter's (sic) wives" is usually changed to "truck drivers' wives" in concert, a change I discuss later. In Dylan's original notebook the lyrics also went through several variations, which I'll also discuss later. I prefer the 1975 version released on "Blood on the Tracks", which is the one that Dylan has preserved in hundreds of concerts largely intact, because it ties together so brilliantly the themes that cut across "Blood on the Tracks" and many other of Dylan's songs, discussed throughout this book.

Just as a reminder, there are the themes of heat and cold - the sun, red hair, stove and coal representing heat, the freezing up and blueness representing cold – symbolic of the heat of love and passion and the cold of despair of lost love. Then there is the bird image – the "bird that flew" - alluded to in chapter 2, which stands as a symbol for the artist or creator.

---

107   For the history behind "Blood on the Tracks", see A. Gill and K. Odegard (2004) *A Simple Twist of Fate: Bob Dylan and the Making of Blood on the Tracks*, De Capo Press. The earlier version was included in the bootleg "Blood on the Track" outtakes which includes several songs from the album, and released on "The Bootleg Series 1-3: Rare and Unreleased 1961-1991".

Then there are the books – Papa's bankbook and the book of poems written in the soul, which self-reflexively point to the other books and words on the album and throughout Dylan's work, discussed in chapter 3. Next there is the contrast between love and money; Papa's bankbook again, as well as the multiple occupations listed on the song – carpenters, mathematicians, cook, fisher, even slave trader. Last there is the much observed playing with time – something again common in many Dylan songs and covered in Chapter 5. But here I discuss the road elements of the song.

Wandering love songs are a standard in ballads, although the multiple lovers implied in "Tangled up in Blue" are perhaps the modern rock star version. The opening lines of "Tangled up in Blue" recall the opening of the famous ballad:

Early one morning, just as the sun was rising,
I heard a maid sing in the valley below[108]

There are numerous secular ballads which start with the traveler setting out and then spying a young maiden he wants for his own. For example, this old British Northumbrian song:

As noble Sir Arthur one morning did ride,

---

[108]   "Early one morning" is also common in the Blues – see Gray p .366. The "valley below" is also used by Dylan in "One More Cup of Coffee". Classics such as "Wandering", recorded by many artists including Josh White Senior, may also have been an influence.

*With his hounds at his feet, and his sword by his
side,
He saw a fair maid sitting under a tree,
He asked her name, and she said 'twas Mollee.*

*'Oh, charming Mollee, you my butler shall be,
To draw the red wine for yourself and for me!
I'll make you a lady so high in degree,
If you will but love me, my charming Mollee! '*

Similarly "The Baffled Knight" which dates from at
least to the seventeenth century:

*There was a knight, and he was young,
A riding along the way, sir,
And there he met a lady fair,
Among the cocks of hay, sir.*

*Quoth he, "Shall you and I, lady,
Among the grass lye down a?
And I will have a special care
Of rumpling of your gown a."*[109]

Friedman comments:

*If a medieval French trouvere or minstrel catered
to a courtly audience, he would be sure to have*

<hr>

[109]   Albert Friedman (ed) *The Penguin Book of Folk Ballads of the
English-Speaking World.*, p. 155. This was first published in 1958, and
contains most of the well-known ballads from which Blues songs, and
subsequently Dylan in "Time out of Mind" and "Love and Theft" drew
much mythical material. For more details on the connection between
the Blues and ballads, see Gray.

in his repertoire a number of pastourelles – short poems describing encounters between a gallant and a shepherdess in the fields or woods, his proposals, her demurrers, his subsequent success or failure. The knight was usually the winner of these aristocratic sex duels, but when the folk took over the form...the story had a different ending. In later centuries, the knight of the early ballads becomes a dragoon, still later, a good soldier; his modern descendant thrives in the traveling-salesman-and-the-farmer's-daughter jokes told in men's clubrooms.[110]

Dylan told one of those traveling salesmen jokes in "Motorpsycho Nightmare", released in 1964:

I pounded on a farmhouse
Lookin' for a place to stay.
I was mighty, mighty tired,
I had gone a long, long way...

I fell down
To my bended knees,
Saying, "I dig farmers,

---

110   ibid p. 148. Benjamin Filene in his book *Romancing the Folk. Public Memory and American Roots Music*. Chapel Hill: University of North Carolina, makes a similar point about Dylan's use of the ballad form. He writes (ibid. p. 219): "Even in his so-called rock period, then, Dylan continued to draw on formal aspects of the folk ballad, but he reassembled these elements in ways that showed less concern with telling story than with playing with the conventions of storytelling. His ballads featured personas that showed the plasticity of persona, morals that questioned the legitimacy of fixed morals, and narratives that demonstrated the breaking down of narrative."

Don't shoot me, please!"
He cocked his rifle
And began to shout,
"You're that travelin' salesman
That I have heard about."
I said, "No! No! No!
I'm a doctor and it's true,
I'm a clean-cut kid
And I been to college, too."

Then in comes his daughter
Whose name was Rita.
She looked like she stepped out of
La Dolce Vita.

And so on. The interesting thing about this early version of "Tangled up in Blue" is that like the latter it jumps right into the song with no introduction: "I pounded on a farmhouse/Lookin' for a place to stay."

"Tangled up in Blue" takes on the simplicity of these early ballads, mainly one syllable words – the way Dylan sings it only "together" and "homemade" from the first verse are two syllables. And no chorus, just the single repeated last line in each verse. These are both characteristics of the first three songs of "Blood on the Tracks", which is why the songs appear to move so swiftly. [111] The short six or seven

111   When Dylan first played the songs to friends they were apparently overwhelmed with the swiftness of their pace – see Gill and Odegard (2004).

syllable lines also follow the patterns of some ballads. Friedmann writes of the ballad style:

> The ballad method of narration is unique, and until one gets used to it, it can be disconcerting. Characteristically a ballad breaks into its story at a moment when the train of action is decisively pointed toward the catastrophe. Setting, time, the appearance of the persons involved, the background, are indicated by a few light strokes or casual hints. Characters pop out of nowhere just at the moment they are needed and are dropped with equal suddenness. We shift from place to place abruptly, scene after scene flashing by without connectives or explanation.[112]

That last sentence is a perfect description of the technique in "Tangled up in Blue" – all we know is that we're on the road shifting from place to place abruptly. As Scobie comments: "the scattered events cannot be convincingly arranged into a logically sequential plot. The best response to the song is to leave the indeterminacy open and to accept that the construction of a conventional story is not one of its purposes."[113] The lineage is a clear one, from British ballads that were transported to the American colony, many of which were compiled in Harry Smith's "Anthology of American Folk Music"

---

112   ibid. p. 148.
113   Scobie p. 268.

which Dylan has drawn on throughout his career.[114] I'll repeat a quote from Primeau which contextualizes this in road travel literature:

> From picaresque tales, the road story gives us rascals and rogues who wander aimlessly to undermine the status quo in episodic adventures that mock acceptable routines and values. Like the picaro antihero, protagonists on the road are cut loose from everyday restraints and of work and daily experiences. As they revel in their wandering, picaro road characters may have difficulty with, or even refuse, reintegration and choose instead to extend their journey indefinitely. [115]

The indefinite journey is one epitomized in "Tangled up In Blue" which ends where it begins. As Ricks points out about another of Dylan's traveling songs, "Song to Woody", released in 1962: "You sense the end is imminent because the song turns back to the beginning...the opening words of the final verse, "I'm a leaving'", recall the opening of the first verse, "I'm out here"...". [116] There's also a repetition of the word "road" in the first and last verses, and the idea of walking aimlessly down the road: "Somewhere

---

114   See Gray for these borrowings. Among the English ballads which became American standards that Dylan has recorded or adapted are " The House Carpenter"; "Lord Randall" – which as Ricks and Gray have shown is a prototype for "A hard rain's a-gonna fall"; "Barbara Allen"; and "Robin Hood and the Monk" – which provides two of the characters for "Desolation Row".
115   p. 7
116   See Ricks, p. 53.

down the road someday". Like "Song to Woody", in "Tangled up in Blue" the repetition of key words in the first and last verses brings us back to the beginning of the song:

> *And I was standin' on the side of the road*
> *Rain fallin' on my shoes*
> *Heading out for the East Coast*
>
> *But me, I'm still on the road*
> *Headin' for another joint*

Always heading, never arriving, "Tangled up in Blue" is different from early ballads because it deals not with reaching a destination or fulfilling a quest, but with being "still on the road", which is why the return in the last verse to the first is so significant. Primeau again:

> *Throughout history, Americans have wandered on horseback, in stagecoaches and wagon trains, on rivers and bicycle paths, and on the modern highway. As Daniel J. Boorstin has reminded us, American migration before and during the frontier experience was movement not in a direct line but in a "churning, casual, vagrant, circular motion around and around."*
> *... The special quality of this movement throughout history offers clues to the restlessness of American culture even now. Whereas most travelers of old in pilgrimages or quest romances moved with deliberation toward goals, Americans were nomadic in their trust*

that the power of movement itself would bring happiness, success and fulfillment…The rootless search for personal and national identity, for example, reaches back at least to Emerson's self-reliance, Thoreau's self-sufficiency, and Whitman's self-celebration.[117]

Andre Peyronie similarly writes about the literary myth of the labyrinth[118]: "During the nineteenth century, the conviction that there was necessarily a path leading to an end died out and, in the space left devoid of its sacred aura, the modern wanderings began. The knights of the Middle Ages meandered through forests under the watchful eye of God, whereas the modern seekers of meaning run the constant risk of indifferent and meaningless peregrinations." Dylan's traveler on "Blood on the Tracks" is constantly on the move, wandering but never arriving – "Me, I'm still on the road"; "Well, I'm livin' in a foreign country but I'm bound to cross the line"; "Hunts her down by the waterfront docks"; "Down the highway, down the tracks, down the road to ecstasy"; "I see a lot of people as I make the rounds/And I hear her name here and there as I go from town to town"; "Honey, we could be in Kansas/By time the snow begins to thaw." The use of the present or future tenses means that Dylan's traveler is a figure perpetually bound to cross the line, but perhaps never getting to cross it.

117   Primeau, pp. 18-19.
118   Peyronie, A. (1992) "The Labyrinth." In P. Brunel (ed) *Companion to Literary Myths, Heroes and Archetypes*. London: Routledge, p. 719.

The road to salvation

Much has been written about Dylan's Christian songs and how these appeared to signify a break from his earlier work, but the road/traveller image is common to these songs too – unsurprising given the symbol of the path so often used in religious writing. Many of the old songs which Dylan drew on in his earlier work also had religious traditions, such as the slaves being led out of darkness by Jesus, and Gray has noted the connection between gospel and the blues.[119] In the Bible (King James version) we find in Matthew 7: 13-14:

> *Enter ye in at the strait gate: for wide is the gate, and broad is the way, that leadeth to destruction, and many there be which go in thereat:*
> *Because strait is the gate, and narrow is the way, which leadeth unto life, and few there be that find it.*

Gates are an important image in Dylan to which we'll return later in this chapter. Here is Dylan's religious road on "What Can I Do For You":

> *I know all about poison, I know all about fiery darts,*
> *I don't care how rough the road is, show me where it starts*

---

119   p. 314, fn. 100.

Here are a few further references from the many in his religious songs:

> *Senor, senor, do you know where we're headin'?*
> *Lincoln County Road or Armageddon?*

> *I'm just going down the road feeling bad*

> *Took an untrodden path once, where the swift*
> *don't win the race,*
> *It goes to the worthy, who can divide the word*
> *of truth....*
> *Noontime, and I'm still pushin' myself along the*
> *road, the darkest part,*
> *Into the narrow lanes, I can't stumble or stay put.*[120]

And so on. I stress continuity here because the road is a symbol of creative and religious quest throughout Dylan's work. The same is true of the train, which is a further traveling image throughout Dylan's work – from the early '60s songs like "Bob Dylan's Dream" and "Honey, Just Allow Me One More Chance", through the mid-60s in "It Takes a Lot to Laugh, It Takes a Train to Cry", "Blood on the Tracks", and the religious imagery of "Slow Train Coming" and the blues imagery of "Tryin' to Get to Heaven" – "People on the platforms/Waiting for the trains" and "Some trains don't pull no gamblers". Train tracks have as much resonance as the path or highway.[121]

---

120   "Senor (Tales of Yankee Power)"; "Tryin' to get to heaven"; "I and I"; "Ye shall be changed".

121   On railways, see Gray, p. 39, 43.

Deep inside my heart/I know I can't escape

Roads, and railway tracks, are also lines that cut through a country, that divide it – on a map, a road is depicted as a line, as in Dylan's "walkin' down the line" or "To stay away from the train line." Like "face", "line" has multiple meanings - the most common uses in Dylan are as a road or train track, a borderline, or a song line, or the shore line, which separates sea from land.[122] Because roads and train tracks are so common in Dylan, and because he exploits so well the multiple meanings of words, Dylan's "lines" are another theme which pulls his work together. The separation created by a border is a key element in Dylan and American literature, and he uses different kinds of borderlines to express this, particularly walls, doors, gates and windows.

Dylan uses the word "line" straightforwardly in the sense of a line of poetry or song, for example:

And there's no use in tryin'
T' deal with the dyin',
Though I cannot explain that in lines.

But Dylan's lines sometimes surprise. When he writes on "I'll Keep it with Mine":

The train leaves
At half past ten,

---

122   The most common usage these days – to be connected to the internet – is not yet used by Dylan in his song lyrics.

But it'll be back tomorrow,
Same time again.
The conductor he's weary,
He's still stuck on the line.

As well as the train line, is he also referring to a musical conductor who's stuck on the line of a score? If he is, this is perhaps the only time he puns so sweetly on "conductor". Also, when he writes on "Tangled up in Blue":

She studied the lines on my face

Is he also thinking about studying the lines of a book (given that "Blood on the Tracks" is a bookish album – see chapter 3)? Because "Studied the lines on my face" is an odd formulation; more normal usage might be "lines of my face". That was the usage Dylan included in the notebook in which he gathered the original lyrics to "Blood on the Tracks".

It's the third use of line – borderline – that is most common in Dylan and directly links lines to roads and travelers. Borders or boundaries have long fascinated writers, because the border is a grey zone where norms change, and they like to explore what is beyond the border, outside the safety of what is known. There is the border between this world and the underworld, crossed by another border, the river Styx; borders between countries, between the country and the city, and between civilization and whatever is outside. Scobie (2003: 32-3) has commented on the trickster figure in Dylan's writing[123]: "The trickster is always in between, in what anthropologists call "liminal" situations…. Prophet and trickster both stand between worlds, crossing borders back and forth, carrying with them their contraband cargo – which may be fire, or even, as Plato suggests, language itself." Crossing the border or the boundary has both physical and spiritual sides.

Gray (2000: 484-5) includes an extensive discussion of lines and borders writing about Dylan's "Brownsville Girl":

> *Border towns are where people cross from one kind of place to another, yet where the conjunction of the two makes for an ill-defined, nebulous entity…When they arrive [after crossing the panhandle] Ruby tells them they've crossed another invisible borderline: "She said 'Welcome to the land of the living dead' . " Next thing we know, with another switch of scene, the narrator feels vulnerable – violent danger seems to loom – even in the act of the smallest crossing: "I was crossin' the street," he says, "when shots rang out." Then, matching the earlier phrase "too over the edge", the women saves him with an alibi is said to have gone "out on a limb" in doing so…The theme is stated most directly and concentratedly in the narrator's protestation that he's "always been the kind of person that doesn't like to trespass, but sometimes you just find yourself over the line."*

---

123   2003: (32-3)

And perhaps not for nothing the song's penultimate verse ends: "I'll stand in line".

How does Dylan use this tradition of travelers and outsiders crossing lines and borders is the question? Brilliantly and with complexity, and perhaps not always in control of his art, is the answer. I referred to "You're a Big Girl Now" in the introduction:

Bird on the horizon, sittin' on a fence,
He's singin' his song for me at his own expense.
And I'm just like that bird, oh, oh,
Singin' just for you

Dylan uses two lines, boundaries or borders here, the horizon and the fence. The singer in this song is not only singing just like the bird, he's also sitting on the fence like the bird. "Sitting on a fence" also has another meaning, someone who is undecided. The singing bird sitting on a fence is common stock in songs and poetry. Leonard Cohen's "Bird on a Wire" – recorded in 1968 - makes a similar connection between the bird, the boundary (in this case apparently a phone wire), and singing. Cohen plays on the multiple meanings of "wire" – the idea of a barbed wire fence, the idea of being on the wireless (coming down the wire), and the idea of being close to the finish (down to the wire). Joni Mitchell uses a similar combination in "Sweet Bird", but the bird is laughing not singing.

And while Dylan's use of boundaries is similar, his bird is quite different from that of Wallace Stevens' in "Of

Mere Being", which is distanced from the human creative process:

The palm at the end of the mind,
Beyond the last thought, rises
In the bronze distance.

A gold-feathered bird
Sings in the palm, without human meaning,
Without human feeling, a foreign song.

Dylan's use of borders and lines is perhaps most intense on "Blood on the Tracks", where his imagery often reaches its peak. Lines crop up in odd places, as in the last verse of "Tangled up in Blue":

So now I'm goin' back again,
I got to get to her somehow.
All the people we used to know
They're an illusion to me now.
Some are mathematicians
Some are carpenter's wives.
Don't know how it all got started,
I don't know what they're doin' with their lives.
But me, I'm still on the road
Headin' for another joint
We always did feel the same,
We just saw it from a different point of view,
Tangled up in blue.

Anyone who has looked closely at Dylan's lyrics will know that he rarely throws in words at random, and of all Dylan's writing it's on "Blood on the Tracks" that word association is at its most concentrated and passionate. "Joint" has multiple meanings. There are two meanings which are easy to figure from previous lines in the song– the joint being the place where you sing or perform (music in the cafes at night, the topless bar – and as used in the first volume of Dylan's autobiography "Chronicles") or the joint you smoke ("She lit a burner on the stove and offered me a pipe"). There are other meanings, for example a prison (as used in Kerouac's "On the Road"). There may also be a reference to a carnival joint.[124] But there's another meaning of joint which relates to lines, which is "an area at which two ends, surfaces, or edges are attached", as in a carpenter's joint, where two lines meet – which is why I prefer Dylan's reference to carpenters rather than truck drivers.[125] In that sense the joint is a boundary the narrator is heading towards, in the sense of heading for a place where he may not be able to cross over. There's a resonance too in rhyming "joint" with "point". When Dylan sings the song "point" hangs at the end of the sentence, and the final rhyme is "view " and "blue". What a cute word to have hanging on the end of the line, because it also has multiple meanings. It is both a full stop (in French a "point" and sometimes referred to in English as a "full point"), and therefore a good word to finish a sentence. It is also an

---

124   Thanks to Mitch Blank for that last reference.
125   As noted, this is a song that has gone through multiple versions. In his notebook for "Blood on the Tracks" Dylan wrote: "Some are mathematicians, some are doctor's wives."

exact moment in time ("at this point"); but also the shortest distance between two points is a straight line, which is presumably why Dylan includes mathematicians among the people they used to know. Subtle wordplay indeed! And reminiscent of another use of "still" and "point" which we will come back to in the chapter on time, from Eliot's "Four Quartets":

At the still point of the turning world.

In the next song on "Blood on the Tracks", "Simple Twist of Fate", Dylan exploits a similar kind of ambiguity when he writes:

Twas then he felt alone and wished that he'd gone straight

He exploits the multiple meanings of to "go straight". There is here both straight in the sense of a "straight line"; of walking straight to something without stopping; and of going straight or stopping illicit activity, the last perhaps intimated by the original lyrics in Dylan's notebook suggesting that the song involves an encounter with a prostitute (see chapter 2). Fortuitous that "straight" rhymes with "fate", but not a fortuitous word – and like so many on "Blood on the Tracks" a word that carries multiple meanings.

On "Idiot Wind" Dylan returns to the borderline. There is the more straightforward usage, punning on "tracks" and returning us to the album's title:

Down the highway, down the tracks, down the road to ecstasy
I followed you beneath the stars, hounded by your memory

The repetition of "down" is not encouraging – as in "going down". Then there is:

I been double-crossed now for the very last time and now I'm finally free,
I kissed goodbye the howling beast on the borderline which separated you from me.[126]

The ambiguous syntax in the second of these lines suggests different meanings. Usually when getting rid of something for good, "I kissed goodbye" would be followed by "to". But Dylan doesn't sing "I kissed goodbye *to* the howling beast", and he pauses when he sings the song on "Blood on the Tracks" to suggest perhaps that he means "kiss goodbye" in the sense of kissing goodbye to say hello again sometime. So it may be that he's not as free as he claims in the previous line, and that borderline – which is a line that's difficult to cross in Dylan's songs – suggests the same. The term "double-crossed" also alludes to both the people Dylan thinks is cheating him, and the difficulty of getting across – as in "I went to tell

---

126   On the outtake, coming back to another theme on "Blood on the Tracks" - cheating - Dylan sings:

I been double-crossed too much
At times I think I've almost lost my mind
Lady killers load dice on me behind my back
While imitators steal me blind

everybody/But I would not get across". Then is he, or the beast, or both, on the borderline?

In "If you See Her, Say Hello" there is another kind of border which it's difficult to get across:

I see a lot of people as I make the rounds
And I hear her name here and there as I go from
town to town

That "round" represents a circle, another kind of line, one which is joined, and to make a round is to go around in a circle.

A song Dylan recorded on "Self Portrait", "Days of '49" includes a similar theme:

Of the comrades all that I've had, there's none
that's left to boast
And I'm left alone in my misery like some poor
wandering ghost
And I pass by from town to town, they call me a
rambling sign
There goes Tom Moore, a bummer sure in the
days of '49.[127]

---

127   An alternative version includes "place" rather than "town":

And now my comrades all are gone,
No one remains to toast,
They have left me here in my misery,
Like some poor wandering ghost,
And as I go from place to place,
Folks call me a "Traveling Sign"
Saying, "There goes Tom Moore, a Bummer, sure,
From the Days of Forty-Nine."

Dylan is aware of the symbolism of circles and their power to entrap, as in the opening lines of "Stuck Inside of Mobile", the image which he borrowed from Joseph Conrad's "The Secret Agent" where Stevie continually draws circles and is unable to talk:

Oh, the ragman draws circles
Up and down the block.
I'd ask him what the matter was
But I know that he don't talk.

A song that goes on to talk about being in a trap:

And the ladies treat me kindly
And furnish me with tape,
But deep inside my heart
I know I can't escape.

The idiot wind on "Blood on the Tracks" is also blowing "like a circle around my skull", all the way to that other circle, the domed Capitol.

The border in its various forms is one to which he returns in "Shelter from the Storm":

I came in from the wilderness, a creature void of form.

Now there's a wall between us, somethin' there's been lost
I took too much for granted, got my signals crossed.

Well, I'm livin' in a foreign country but I'm bound to cross the line
Beauty walks a razor's edge, someday I'll make it mine.

In the last quote, as in the lines above from "You're a Big Girl Now", there are two kinds of borders, the line he's bound to cross, and that thinnest of borders, the razor's edge. "Cross" in the third quote refers back to both the signals being "crossed", also to being double crossed and the "lone soldier on the cross" in "Idiot Wind" – "Shelter from the Storm" itself being a song full of Christian religious imagery.[128]

Being "bound to cross the line" also plays with the multiple meanings of bound, both boundary and movement, as in Guthrie's "Bound for Glory". As a noun and transitive verb it means to confine or restrain or tie up, or, figuratively, to oblige. As an intransitive verb it means to leap. There's a passage in Milton's "Paradise Lost" which plays on the double meaning of the word "bound" in the same way as Dylan. Milton describes Satan leaping the gates of Eden:

One gate there only was, and that looked east
On the other side. Which when the Arch-Felon saw,

---

128   This is an unusual use of crossed signals, because a single person can't get their signals crossed. There is also the reference to train signals, and to the sign of the cross, from where this phrase may have originated.

> *Due entrance he disdained, and, in contempt,*
> *At one slight bound high overleaped all bound*

Dylan writes:

> *Well, I'm livin' in a foreign country but I'm bound*
> *to cross the line*

Milton writes:

> *At one slight bound high overleaped all bound*

But, quite different from Milton, the point about Dylan's borders and lines is how difficult they are to cross – he isn't crossing the line here, he's bound to cross it, similar to being still, on the road. As in that "joint" to which he is heading, which is a dead end; like the conductor, who's still stuck on the line; like the bird sitting on a fence; like the lover making the rounds. The line may take the traveller somewhere, but it's a difficult line to cross, and may not lead anywhere after all except maybe the world's end.

Someone to open each and every door: doors, windows, halls and gates

That passage from "Paradise Lost" goes on to discuss other kinds of borders, using similes to describe Satan's transgressions:

> *At one slight bound high overleaped all bound*
> *Of hill or highest wall, and sheer within*

Lights on his feet. As when a prowling wolf,
Whom hunger drives to seek new haunt for prey,
Watching where shepherds pen their flocks at eve,
In hurdled cotes amid the field secure,
Leaps o'er the fence with ease into the fold;
Or as a thief, bent to unhoard the cash
Of some rich burgher, whose substantial doors,
Cross-barred and bolted fast, fear no assault,
In at the window climbs, or o'er the tiles;
So climbs this first grand Thief into God's fold.[129]

"Paradise Lost" is a poem about different kinds of transgressions, crossing different kinds of physical and moral boundaries, which foreshadows Dylan uses. At the end of the poem Adam and Eve head to the gates of Eden which Satan leapt over, and in the final lines of the poem become solitary wanderers (the first wandering lonesome travelers?):

The world was all before them, where to choose
Their place of rest, and Providence their guide.
They, hand in hand, with wandering steps and slow,
Through Eden took their solitary way.

---

129   Coincidentally (or not?) Dylan wrote on "Handy Dandy":

"He's got that clear crystal fountain
He's got that soft silky skin
He's got that fortress on the mountain
With no doors, no windows, no thieves can break in".

Among the most common images in Dylan's songs are the door, the window, the gate and the hallway. Like the lines and the tracks, they are usually barriers or boundaries that separate the singer from others, or that prevent his moving on, or creating. So common is their use – and perhaps now their overuse – that they are another common poetic denominator of Dylan's songs. It would be odd to hear a Dylan song which didn't have a highway, door or a window in it. And there is a very particular relation between barriers and the wind which Dylan frequently draws on to set up a tension in his songs between freedom/movement/ creativity and stasis, in a similar way that the road or the line represents both a trap and place to wonder.

As we saw in chapter 2, "Blonde on Blonde", released in 1966, is an album about waiting, about doors, and about impassable gates. The image of the door adds to the sense of claustrophobia and no escape. "Temporary Like Achilles" is a song organized around doors and walls:

Standing on your window, honey,
Yes, I've been here before.
Feeling so harmless,
I'm looking at your second door.

Kneeling 'neath your ceiling,
Yes, I guess I'll be here for a while….
How come you send someone out to have me barred?

> Well, I rush into your hallway,
> Lean against your velvet door.
> I watch upon your scorpion
> Who crawls across your circus floor.

"Standing on your window" – what's that meant to mean? Who even gave Dylan permission to write that kind of stuff?

This is followed immediately by "Absolutely Sweet Marie":

> Well, your railroad gate, you know I just can't jump it
> Sometimes it gets so hard, you see
> I'm just sitting here beating on my trumpet

Those damned railroad gates - nothing worse than them to keep the sex-craved lover out.

The atmospheric opening to 'Visions of Johanna" *is established by the claustrophobic room, another kind of trap:*

> Lights flicker from the opposite loft
> In this room the heat pipes just cough

Which is repeated in "Pledging my Time":

> Well, the room is so stuffy,
> I can hardly breathe.

As Scobie has noted:

> *Dylan's songs are full of rooms...often, again they are places that he has left behind and looks back to. ...Rooms are places of danger... or of betrayal... the room may even be the site of death....As late as "Time Out of Mind", the room is still a dominant image, still associated with restriction and abandonment. "I've been pacing round the room, hoping maybe she come back'" he sings in "Dirt Road Blues." "I've been praying round for salvation, laying round in a one-room country shack." Most ominously in "Not Dark Yet," "there not even room enough to be anywhere." Here "room" is the very condition of existence, and it too has been taken away.*[130]

Dylan and doors

Doors operate in a similar way to gates in Dylan's songs. There is one Dylan song where someone walks through the door to get to the other side which I quote below, but otherwise he's knocking on the door, rapping at the door, standing in the doorway, trying to get through the door before it's closed – here's a selection from throughout Dylan's writing career:

> *Oh, sister, when I come to knock on your door*

> *You gave me a map and a key to your door*

---

130   Scobie, p. 46.

I can hear the turning of the key
Babe, I couldn't find the door

He come in to the door, he couldn't get in

I received your letter yesterday
(About the time the doorknob broke)[131]

Go away from my door and my window too

Closed the door behind him

And the station doors are closed.

How long must I keep my eyes glued to the door

They'll stone ya when you're walkin' to the door

Every time I crawl past your door

I walked down the hallway
And I heard his door slam

Though I tried and failed at finding any door[132]

---

131   A sweet use of the preposition "about". Is the letter about the doorknob breaking, or was the letter received at about the time the doorknob broke? I know the letter is meant to be about something meaningless, but I can't help admiring Dylan prepositioning. He does this many times (see my comments on "rapping on your door" below).
132   "Oh, Sister"; "Sara"; "Abandoned Love"; "If Not for You"; "Oxford Town"; "Desolation Row"; "Bob Dylan's Blues"; "George Jackson"; "Meet Me in the Morning"; "Senor"; "Rainy Day Women #12 & 35"; "Idiot Wind"; "Percy's Song"; "Love is Just a Four Letter Word".

Freud wrote: "Anyone who has had experience in the translating of dreams will, of course, at once be reminded that penetration into narrow spaces and the opening of locked doors are among the commonest of sexual symbols…".[133] – which makes the line from "Absolutely Sweet Marie" even more obvious:

> *Yes, I can take him to your house but I can't unlock it*
> *You see, you forgot to leave me with the key*

A reminder that Dylan's songs are not about opening doors comes in "It Ain't Me, Babe"

> *Go 'way from my window,*
> *Leave at your own chosen speed.*
> *I'm not the one you want, babe,*
> *I'm not the one you need.*
> *You say you're lookin' for someone*
> *Never weak but always strong,*
> *To protect you an' defend you*
> *Whether you are right or wrong,*
> *Someone to open each and every door…*

Not just to open the door, but to open each and every door.

The phrasing on doors from "It's All Over Now, Baby Blue" is interesting:

---

133   "The Interpretation of Dreams". Translated by A.A. Brill. Plain Label Books, 1911. For Dylan's use of sexual language, see chapter 2.

The vagabond who's rapping at your door
Is standing in the clothes that you once wore.

The threat of the stranger/outsider it reinforced by the word "rapping" and the idea – borne through from "Like A Rolling Stone" that one day whoever is being addressed may themselves be a vagabond. The more common usage would be "Rapping on" or "Knocking on" – rapping **at** includes alliteration which makes it more violent. This is perhaps taken from Poe's "The Raven":

But the fact is I was napping, and so gently you came rapping,
And so faintly you came tapping, tapping at my chamber door.[134]

Given the context of the poem and its other-wordly nature, Poe probably had in mind the idea of "spirit rapping" or communication with the dead, some-thing Dylan may have had in mind too in the line that precedes those just quoted:

Forget the dead you've left, they will not follow you.

OK, there is at least one Dylan song where the narrator gets to go through a door, but it doesn't

---

134   The inspiration might also be Blind Willie McTell's "Broke Down Engine" which includes the line: "Don't you hear me baby: rapping on your door".

lead anywhere promising, and anyway, it's just in a dream –Bob Dylan's 115th:

> *I ran right through the front door*
> *Like a hobo sailor does*
> *But it was just a funeral parlor*
> *And the man asked me who I was*

In using doors so frequently to express entrapment and boundaries that, like borderlines, can't be crossed, Dylan draws on a theme common to other writers, another common poetic denominator. There's a similar tension in Poe's short stories, where there is a continual coming and going between freedom and entrapment. In story after story Poe writes about tombs, vaults, chambers and traps, both physical and mental. The tension between freedom and entrapment is another theme in Henry James' *Portrait of a Lady*, with Isabel Archer meditating on the trap of her marriage and perhaps returning to that confinement at the end of her novel. But there is another kind of use of doors in modern western literature, to suggest movements from one state to another. Fontana noted:

> *Doors are passages that… suggest barriers, often barriers of the self, but also entrances, which when they terminate poems as in Hopkins's "In Honour of St. Alphonsus Rodriguez" or stanzas as in Christina Rossetti's "Echo", suggest, particularly when they rhyme with more, evermore or*

before, an entrance into a desired, anticipated, or remembered dimension of visionary time.[135]

Fontana goes on: "[the] common English rhyme of door and more requires a signification of transition from one state to another that differ from each other in quantity. Often, particularly in Dickinson, the other state lies beyond the walled or enclosed room of the self."[136] This is a rhyme Dylan uses in at least 10 songs at line endings, and also for internal rhymes, such as in "Idiot Wind" and "Desolation Row":

I can't feel you anymore, I can't even touch the books you've read
Every time I crawl past your door, I been wishin' I was somebody else instead.

Yes, I received your letter yesterday
(About the time the door knob broke)
... Right now I can't read too good
Don't send me no more letters no

Although nineteenth century English poets may have used the rhyme "more" and "door" to signify a transition, in Dylan it is a rhyme which signifies either closure or movement to a worse scenario, as in "Tryin' to Get to Heaven":

---

135   Ernest L Fontana. "Victorian Doors". *Philosophy and Literature*. 2006.Vol.30 (1), p.284. This article gives a number of usages of "door' in English 19th century poetry. The more/door rhyme is common in the blues.
136   Fontana, p. 277.

You broke a heart that loved you
Now you can seal up the book and not write
anymore
I've been walking that lonesome valley
Trying to get to heaven before they close the
door

When you think that you lost everything
You find out you can always lose a little more
I'm just going down the road feeling bad
Trying to get to heaven before they close the
door

The first two lines of the second stanza are reminiscent of Shakespeare's "King Lear" a play Dylan adapted before, in "Tears of Rage". Those lines from "Tryin' to Get to Heaven" recall:

And worse I may be yet. The worst is not
So long as we can say 'This is the worst.'[137]

Leonard Cohen uses a room, a door and the difficulty of communication in "Love Itself". In this song the singer is inside a little room, with love leaving, also exploiting the common "more/door" rhyme.

Emily Dickinson similarly uses the door/more rhyme to signify closure rather than movement to a new state, as in "We never know we go when we are going-":

---

137   Act IV, Scene I.

We never know we go when we are going-
We jest and shut the Door-
Fate-following-behind us bolts it-
And we accost no more-[138]

As Fontana notes, going through the door can be a form of literary freedom. We can see how different Dylan is from Whitman, who writes in "Song of Myself", lines unimaginable in a Dylan song:

Unscrew the locks from the doors!
Unscrew the doors themselves from their jambs!

Nor can Dylan repeat the raw sexuality of Memphis Minnie – another influence – who sings on "Bumble Bee" about a stinging bumblebee that flies in through the door.

Nor does he write like Springsteen on "Leah":

I got somethin' in my heart, I been waitin' to give
I got a life I wanna start, one I been waitin' to live
No more waitin', tonight I feel the light I say the prayer
I open the door, I climb the stairs...

More similar perhaps to a poet we know influenced Dylan, Allen Ginsberg, who ends "Howl":

I'm with you in Rockland

---

138   Quoted in Fontana.

in my dreams you walk dripping from a sea -
journey on the highway across America in tears
to the door of my cottage in the Western night

The ambiguous ending of a journey at a door is closer to Dylan's use of the boundary.

If doors are everywhere in Dylan's songs, so too are another kind of barrier, windows. Much of what I've written about doors holds true for windows, except because of the more difficult rhyme perhaps Dylan uses these symbols less often. If doors open up onto another world or the unconscious, then the eyes are the "window of the soul". There's plenty of looking, staring and gazing out of windows in Dylan's songs, even, as quoted from "Temporary like Achilles", standing on windows. But like the door, the window symbolizes something which it isn't possible to go beyond.[139] In "Simple Twist of Fate" the window is used as a symbol reflecting back on lost love:

He woke up, the room was bare
He didn't see her anywhere.
He told himself he didn't care, pushed the window open wide,
Felt an emptiness inside

---

139   Although a window is not something you usually go through (or crawl through) unless trying to escape in a hurry, as in "I Shall be Free":

I hot-footed it . . . bare-naked . . .
Out the window!

"I Dreamed I Saw St. Augustine" ends:

Oh, I awoke in anger,
So alone and terrified,
I put my fingers against the glass
And bowed my head and cried.[140]

And in the haunting "Blind Willie McTell", Dylan closes the song:

I'm gazing out the window
Of the St. James Hotel
And I know no one can sing the blues
Like Blind Willie McTell

Ricks writes of this ending: "I admire and love the way in which this claims so little even perhaps claims nothing, does no more than report one of those moments when, abstracted from evil, you gaze out of a window in contemplative regard that is not self-regard."[141] But perhaps there is more happening here, because in Dylan gazing out the window suggests not only contemplation but the complexities and challenges of creation, as in the link between gazing out the window and singing the blues, and which we come to now.

---

140   Dylan's liner notes to "John Wesley Harding", on which "I Dreamed I Saw St. Augustine" features, includes a story where the one character, Frank, who supposedly has the key to the meaning of the album, interpets it thus: "Then he took a deep breath, moaned and punched his fist through the plate-glass window." I'll read this as a negative comment on those who try to analyse Dylan's songs!
141   *Dylan's Visions of Sin*, p. 73.

Wind and windows

No surprise perhaps that songwriters and poets like to use "wind" and "window" together, given the etymology of "window", a mix of wind and eye, or an eye hole through which to see the wind. Where you find a line or a highway or a road or a door or a window in Dylan's songs, you often find its antithesis, the wind, or breath or songs, or creation. It's the same tension I noted earlier when discussing highways, between creating and being trapped (ain't talking, just walking), and between moving and standing still.

As I noted in chapter 3, in English romantic poetry the wind is usually associated with liberation of the spirit and freedom, and the wind also often stands as a symbol of creativity. There is also a close association between the elements outside and the poet's internal feelings. The idea of the wind hitting on a border comes up in an early Dylan song, "Girl from the North Country":

> Well, if you're travelin' in the north country fair,
> Where the winds hit heavy on the borderline,
> Remember me to one who lives there.
> She once was a true love of mine.

There's probably a Blues influence here, for example from Garfield Akers "Cottonfield Blues":

> I'm going to write you a letter: I'm going to mail it in the sky

Mama I know you going to catch it: when the
wind blows on the line

There's also, probably, a pun here intended on
"line", given that the wind is carrying the letter, and
note the similar combination in Dylan of the wind,
the line and passing on a message of love. Sleepy
John Estes, another Blues influence on Dylan, deals
with similar themes on "Jack and Jill Blues".

There are some quite straightforward uses of "wind"
or weather blowing around the door or the window in Dylan's songs, for example "On a Night Like
This", "Walls of Red Wing" and "Tweedle Dee and
Tweedle Dum":

Let the four winds blow
Around this old cabin door,
If I'm not too far off
I think we did this once before.
There's more frost on the window glass
With each new tender kiss
Storm clouds are raging all around my door

The night aimed shadows
Through the crossbar windows,
And the wind punched hard
To make the wall-siding sing.

Well, the rain beating down on my windowpane
I got love for you and it's all in vain
Then there is a more complicated, and much dis-
cussed use, in "Love Minus Zero/No Limit" – as we

have seen in chapter 3, a song like so many of Dylan's about the difficulties of communication – which ends with these lines:

The bridge at midnight trembles,
The country doctor rambles,
Bankers' nieces seek perfection,
Expecting all the gifts that wise men bring.
The wind howls like a hammer,
The night blows cold and rainy,
My love she's like some raven
At my window with a broken wing.

Ricks has written of the last lines[142]:

The violence that had been disavowed in the beginning ["My love she speaks like silence/ Without ideals or violence"] has come to constitute the end. For violence is just below the surface of the lines:

The wind howls like a hammer
The night blows rainy[143]

All but silently (that is, tacitly), this invokes the raining of blows on somebody with a hammer. When "rain" and "blows" and "hammer" go together, "perfection" is set to meet "hammer", without rhyme but with reason.

---

142   Dylan's Visions of Sin, pp 301.
143   Ricks also discusses the various versions of this line Dylan uses. The version I quote is from bobdylan.com.

But perhaps there is more to say about these lines. The construction is so brilliant – the alliteration in howl, blow, cold, window, broken, the absence of the verb in the final two lines (which should read "my love she's like some raven sitting at my window with a broken wing" or something like that); and the inversion of the last sentence, with window coming between the raven and the broken wing, where we might expect a broken pane, given the hammering wind, but which suggests vulnerability of both the window and his love. And shouldn't it be the wind blowing, not the night?

Dylan was likely also remembering Poe's "The Raven" when writing this song, not only the idea of some ghostly raven outside the window, but a poem which also starts at midnight and the use of "wind" and "window",[144]:

Back into the chamber turning, all my soul within me burning,
Soon again I heard a tapping somewhat louder than before.
'Surely,' said I, 'surely that is something at my window lattice;
Let me see then, what thereat is, and this mystery explore -

---

144   In "Chronicles" (p. 37), Dylan writes about his time in Greenwich village in the early 1960s: "I read the poetry books, mostly, Byron, and Shelley and Longfellow and Poe. I memorized Poe's poem "The Bells" and strummed it to a melody on my guitar."

Let my heart be still a moment and this mystery explore; -
'Tis the wind and nothing more!'

Creation, silence, birds, midnight or later, the wind and the window are themes used in combination by many artists. There is something perversely attractive about creating late at night when sitting by a window with a storm or wind outside. And Dylan's use of "window" as a kind of barrier is also common.

Let's start with Seamus Heaney in his "Elegy" for Robert Lowell in "Field Work":

the sill geranium is lit
by the lamp I write by,
a wind from the Irish Sea
is shaking it—

…Two a.m., seaboard weather.

…And now a teem of rain
and the geranium tremens.

Kipling is also up past his bedtime at the window in "The Dawn Wind":

At two o'clock in the morning, if you open your window and listen,
You will hear the feet of the Wind that is going to call the sun.

*And the trees in the shadow rustle and the trees
in the moonlight glisten,
And though it is deep, dark night, you feel that
the night is done.*

*So do the cows in the field. They graze for an
hour and lie down,
Dozing and chewing the cud; or a bird in the ivy
wakes,
Chirrups one note and is still, and the restless
Wind strays on,
Fidgeting far down the road, till, softly, the dark-
ness breaks.*

What is it with these poets being up at 2 in the morning? Get some sleep guys, you'll feel less ugly in the
morning. Lowell himself wasn't adverse to late night
storm watching, in "Window" from "The Dolphin":

*Tops of the midnight trees move helter-skelter
to ruin, if passion can hurt the classical
in the limited window of the easel painter-
love escapes our hands. We open the curtains:
a square of white-faced houses swerving,
foaming:
the swagger of the world and the chalk of
London.
At each turn the houses wall the path of meeting,
and yet we meet, stand taking in the storm.*

Here is Emily Dickinson, in "The Storm" [145]:

There came a wind like a bugle;
It quivered through the grass,
And a green chill upon the heat
So ominous did pass
We barred the windows and the doors
As from an emerald ghost

Wallace Stevens in "Domination in Black" uses the same themes as Dylan in "Love Minus Zero/No Limit" of the window, the wind, the night and the bird.

Out of the window,
I saw how the planets gathered
Like the leaves themselves
Turning in the wind.
I saw how the night came,
Came striding like the color of the heavy hemlocks,
I felt afraid.
And I remembered the cry of peacocks.

And there is Dylan up late, leaning on the window, wanting to "tell" everyone something; but unable to communicate – and something of an insomniac as we will see in the next chapter on time - on "It Takes a Lot to Laugh, It Takes a Train to Cry":

---

[145]   Perhaps the source of Dylan's line in "Lay Down Your Weary Tune":

The morning breeze like a bugle blew
Against the drums of dawn.

Well, I ride on a mailtrain, baby,
Can't buy a thrill.
Well, I've been up all night, baby,
Leanin' on the window sill.

...Now the wintertime is coming,
The windows are filled with frost.
I went to tell everybody,
But I could not get across.

I could go on, but, point made?[146] What do all these quotes have in common, and have in common with Dylan's use in "Love Minus Zero/No Limit"? Wind and window play together, the latter protection from the former and the storm that it brings – ghosts, storms, or birds. That a song with a title "No Limit" ends with a symbol that is often a barrier is ironic. Like the door or the room or the borderline, the window is used in Dylan as a barrier that cannot be crossed. In a way Dylan perhaps could not have written, Larkin's "High Windows" reflects on a quite different kind of window, one of escape and the wonder beyond it, of boundaries pushed aside rather than entrapment, and one that also includes, like "Love Minus Zero" the relation between words and silence, wind/air and free birds. But maybe Larkin is similar to Dylan, because the poem ends by going beyond words into end-

---

146   See also Robert Frost's "Wind and Window Flower" and "Now Close the Windows", Keats' "The Eve of St. Agnes" and Yeats' "Mad as the Mist and Snow".

less nowhere, just like Dylan's "last outback at the world's end":

> *That'll be the life;*
> *No God any more, or sweating in the dark*
>
> *About hell and that, or having to hide*
> *What you think of the priest. He*
> *And his lot will all go down the long slide*
> *Like free bloody birds. And immediately*
>
> *Rather than words comes the thought of high windows:*
> *The sun-comprehending glass,*
> *And beyond it, the deep blue air, that shows*
> *Nothing, and is nowhere, and is endless.*

The end of the highway has been reached and there is only one thing beyond – endless nothing and nowhere. Let's move to the endless now. Because time is money, and because time is a jet plane, and because time is an ocean which lies at the shore, and because most of the time Dylan writes about time, our last chapter covers our best enemy and worst friend, and what more fitting way to close a book than to end on time?

CHAPTER 5

Dylan, once upon a time

Dylan obsesses about time like only a modern writer can, because time, even more than love, has been *the* constant preoccupation of modern western literature – time passes slowly, the times they are a changing, modern times, born in time.... As Scobie notes in relation to "Time Out of Mind" (referring firstly to "Tryin' to Get to Heaven"):

> Theologically, the only definitive "closing" of heaven's door would be at the Last Judgement; and familiar Dylan images of the Apocalypse recur – in "Can't Wait," "the end of time has begun;" in "Not Dark Yet," "time is running away." Again this apprehension of time coming to a drastic end, the singer sets his pleas to "stop time." In "Love Sick" he hears the clock tick, and in "Highlands" he asks, "I wish someone would come and push back the clock for me.[147]

---

147   P. 300

Meyerhoff makes a cogent argument about the importance of time in modern literature:

> And "once upon a time" is the "timeless" theme of every story told by man, from fairy tales to the opening sentence of the Portrait of the Artist as a Young Man. To be engaged in literature, therefore, quite naturally leads to questions about the meaning of time for the art form itself. Moreover, if art holds a mirror up to human nature, and if man is more conscious than he was of the pervasive and precarious nature of time, then this consciousness will be reflected increasingly in literary works.
>
> This is borne out in the writing of our own age. Time has become, as Wyndham Lewis was perhaps the first to point out, an over-all and predominant theme in recent literature.[148]

Recently Dylan has been thinking about time in relation to his album titles: "Time Out of Mind", "Modern Times", "Together Through Life". But is there a Dylan song that doesn't have some sort of reference to time? As he deals with the highway, writing, and love, Dylan writes about time, sleep, insomnia, wasting time, and transcending time, in the most interesting ways, and time themes have structured his writing from its beginning, so that, to paraphrase Eliot,

---

148   Meyerhoff, H. (1968) *Time in Literature*. Berkeley: University of California Press, 3.

with whom we will begin and end, in his beginning is his end.

These days we're all self-imposed slaves to time in one way or another:

People on the platforms
Waiting for the trains
I can hear their hearts a-beatin'
Like pendulums swinging on chains[149]

Like a pendulum, or like a clock ticking, because since their discovery around 1658 until not that long ago the motion of pendulums was used for time-keeping, and was the world's most accurate time-keeping technology until the 1930s.[150] How about that twitterish summing up the human condition in 20 words (or less), the monotonous clickety clack of the train keeping time with the pendulum measuring out our own time in hearbeats. Not for nothing our hearts are known as "tickers". "Waiting" is a key Dylan word when it comes to writing about time, nowhere more so than on "Blonde on Blonde" which we'll look at too in this chapter.

The way we often think about time is culturally determined by modernity - and different from the way in which time had been previously conceptualized. Our idea of a "good night's sleep" – or eight hours of deep uninterrupted sleep – contrasts with sleep

---

149   "Tryin' to get to heaven".
150   http://en.wikipedia.org/wiki/Pendulum

patterns through history which involved waking periods through the night to pray or work.[151] It's common to talk about ancient Greek, Buddhist and Hindu conceptions of time as cyclical, rather than as linear in the Christian tradition. Medieval concepts of time included history as concurrent – that is, the Trojan war was seen as taking place at the same time as Arthurian quests.

E.P. Thompson argues (in the appropriately titled journal *Past and Present* – and who better than a Marxist historian to dissect a concept that involves people as active participants in their own oppression) that our linear sense of time is quite different from that of rural people in developing countries, at least until recently. Thompson quotes Bourdieu on rural Algerians' nonchalant indifference to the passage of time which no one dreams of mastering, using up, or saving; haste is seen as a lack of decorum combined with diabolical ambition. He quotes as well Evans-Pritchard on the "fortunate" Nuer who never experience the same feeling of fighting against time as people in modern western society, or of having to co-ordinate activities with an abstract passage of time, because their points of reference are mainly the activities themselves, which are generally of a leisurely character.

How then in modern western society did time become money? It's an important question for writers like

---

151   Summers-Bremmer, E. (2008) *Insomnia: A Cultural History*. London: Reaktion Books.

Dylan who have explored what time = money has meant for people trying to live human and humane lives. Thompson suggests that pre-1800[152]:

> we get the characteristic irregularity of labour patterns before the coming of large-scale machine-powered industry. Within the general demands of the week's or fortnight's tasks — the piece of cloth, so many nails or pairs of shoes — the working day might be lengthened or shortened....

Thompson argues that the work pattern pre-1800 was one of alternate bouts of intense labour and of idleness. The irregularity of the working day and week were framed, until the first decades of the nineteenth century, within the larger irregularity of the working year, punctuated by its traditional holidays, and fairs.

Modern time (or modern times) in contrast has nothing romantic, irregular, seasonal or timeless about it, being based on our exploiting time, in the time money equation, where busyness has become identical to business. Thompson argues that new concepts of time were introduced to ensure work discipline among factory workers now destined to clock in and work shifts to ensure maximum profits for their employers. The irregular labour rhythms described in the previous section are replaced by:[153]

---

152   (1967) "Time, Work Discipline and Industrial Capital." In *Past and Present*, 38 (1), 71.
153   p. 90.

the division of labour; the supervision of labour; fines; bells and clocks; money incentives; preachings and schoolings; the suppression of fairs and sports —.new labour habits were formed, and a new time-discipline was imposed. It sometimes took several generations (as in the Potteries), and we may doubt how far it was ever fully accomplished: irregular labour rhythms were perpetuated (and even institutionalized) into the present century, notably in London and in the great ports

Thompson goes on to argue that in capitalist society all time must be consumed, marketed, and put to use, and that it is offensive for the labour force merely to pass the time. Thompson points to Dickens' character Thomas Gradgrind as symbolic of this new time -"ready to weigh and measure any parcel of human nature, and tell you exactly what it comes to" the "deadly statistical clock" in his observatory, "which measured every second with a beat like a rap upon a coffin-lid".

Dylan has something similar to say himself in "Chronicles", about different perceptions of time in America:[154]

There was a difference in the concept of time, too. In the South, people lived their lives with sun-up, high moon, sunset, spring, summer. In the North, people lived by the clock. The factory stroke, whistles and bells. Northerners had to 'be

---

154   "Chronicles", p. 86.

on time'. In some ways the Civil War would be a battle between two kinds of time.

And in some ways Dylan's songs are also about the battle between two kinds of time, clock time and the poetic moment which aims to transcend time. One task that poets set themselves, and one of the roles of literature, of art, culture and song, is to take us beyond our linear sense of time into a zone where time and space become one, where we move into a realm of timeless well-being. How does Dylan fare?

Well, I've been up all night baby, leanin' on the window sill

We've already seen how poets and singers like to imagine themselves on the borders of wakefulness and sleep, gazing out of the window (another border) at birds singing back to them – "Well it's four in the morning by the sound of the birds/I'm starin' at your picture, I'm hearin' your words." ("Under Your Spell"). Maybe it's the peripatetic late night rock star scene, and I don't think he ever uses the word insomnia, but Dylan writes a lot about staying up all night. Here's "Sugar Baby" from the 2001 album "Love and Theft":

I see the morning light
Well' it's not because
I'm an early riser
I didn't go to sleep last night

Not an early riser, but perhaps an early waker who likes to write about sleep, as in those familiar lines from "Tangled up in Blue":

Early one morning the sun was shining
And I was lying in bed.

There's an interesting semi-comic story in "Chronicles" where Dylan recounts the recording of "Oh Mercy":

After being in New Orleans for about a month, I was up early and I rooted my wife out of bed. Daylight was two hours away. "What's wrong now?" she said. I hadn't thought that anything was wrong.

There's sleeplessness when you're in love, as in "You Angel You":

You know I can't sleep at night for trying,
Never did feel this way before.
I get up at night and walk the floor.
If this is love then gimme more
And more and more and more and more.

There's more of the same on "Spirit on the Water" from ""Modern Times" in 2006:

Spirit on the water
Darkness on the face of the deep
I keep thinking about you baby
I can't hardly sleep

Then there's sleepiness when you're in love, as in "New Morning":

The night passed away so quickly
It always does when you're with me.

What better thing for the night to do when a new morning is just around the corner. But surely it should be: "the night passed by so quickly" – or has night got fed up with playing tricks and finally died? Dylan seemed to be sleeping well on "New Morning", because he writes about it again on "If Not For You":

If not for you,
Babe, I'd lay awake all night,
Wait for the mornin' light
To shine in through,
But it would not be new,
If not for you.

Then there's the love involved in wanting to stay up all night, as in "Lay Lady Lay":

Lay, lady, lay, lay across my big brass bed
Stay, lady, stay, stay while the night is still ahead
I long to see you in the morning light
I long to reach for you in the night
Stay, lady, stay, stay while the night is still ahead

He's up before dawn again in "Don't Think Twice, It's All Right"

When your rooster crows at the break of dawn
Look out your window and I'll be gone

Wakefulness caused by erratic love was a popular theme in the Blues, for example Ma Rainey's "Those All Night Long Blues", recorded in 1923:

I just lay and suffer, crying, sighing all night long
'Cause the way that I'm worried, Lordy it sure is
wrong
All night long, all night long
It's this one man on my mind
Can't sleep a wink at night from crying
All night long, got my worries just renewed
And I suffer with those all night blues

Dylan does the same kind of thing on a blues standard (recorded by Muddy Waters and many others), "Rollin' and Tumblin' ", which he recorded on "Modern Times" in 2006:

I rolled and I tumbled, I cried the whole night
long
I rolled and I tumbled, I cried the whole night
long

And again on "Call Letter Blues", an outtake from "Blood on the Tracks" released in 1991 on the first 3 volumes of the bootleg series[155]:

---

155   On "Call Letter Blues" and the blues influence on this song, see Gray (2004: 375ff).

Well, I walked all night long
Listenin' to them church bells tone
Yes, I walked all night long
Listenin' to them church bells tone
Either someone needing mercy
Or maybe something I've done wrong

In a more downbeat reference, on "Forgetful Heart" released in 2009 on "Together through Life", Dylan writes about laying awake and returns to the familiar image of the closed door (with reverberations of Edgar Allen Poe in "the Raven"), but with a twist:

Forgetful heart
Like a walking shadow in my brain
All night long
I lay awake and listen to the sound of pain
The door has closed forevermore
If indeed there ever was a door

Dylan doesn't often write about writing during the night, but he does write about being kept awake by images, intriguingly in "Visions of Johanna":

How can I explain?
Oh, it's so hard to get on
And these visions of Johanna, they kept me up past the dawn

We're not done there in this song, because along with the whispering all-night girls we hear:

....the night watchman click his flashlight
Ask himself if it's him or them that's really insane

"All-night girls"? Since when was "all-night" an adjective (or even a word)? But as we've seen in chapter 2 in the case of "Sad-Eyed Lady of the Lowlands", one of Dylan's favorite ploys on "Blonde on Blonde" is to use nouns as adjectives. Dylan's fabricated noun "all-night" is brilliant in synthesizing what those girls get up to all night. Both this and the night watchman take us back to the first line where the night is playing tricks — and it's the night which the night watchman is presumably watching.[156]

Night watchmen come up from time to time in poetry. One of Shakespeare's insomnia sonnets, "Is it thy will thy image should keep open", includes:

It is my love that keeps mine eye awake,
Mine own true love that doth my rest defeat
To play the watchman ever for thy sake.
For thee watch I whilst thou doest wake elsewhere,
Form me far off, with others all too near.

Marina Tsveraeva, another notorious insomniac, included the following in one of her all-night poems:

---

156   Presumably Dylan was not referring to the game of cricket where a nightwatchman is a lower-order batsman who comes in to bat higher up the order than usual near the end of the day's play.

Once asleep – who knows if we'll wake again?
We have time, we have time, we have time to
sleep!
From house to house the sharp-eyed
watchman goes with his pink lantern
and over the pillow scatters the rattle
of his loud clapper, rumbling.

And – last example here but I could have included more, Robert Frost wanders the night in "Acquainted with the Night" only to wander by a night watchman.[157]

Staying awake through passion or the urge to create are common themes in the poetry of many societies. In the introduction to her anthology of insomnia poems, Lisa Russ Spaar writes:

Like other notorious literary insomniacs – Marcel Proust, Charles Dickens, Elizabeth Bishop, Yannis Ritsos, Nabokov wanted, literally and artistically, to be an eye awake – a seer – in a sleeping world, a solitary watcher among the unconscious. The word watch derives from the Old English watc-can, to be or stay awake, to keep vigil, and in many of these poems, the speaker, eyes open, is a lone keeper of awareness. Abandoned by sleep, and by those who have surrendered to its oblivion, these poets find themselves engaged

---

157   When I stayed in Dhaka in Bangladesh several times in the 1990s I would hear the night guards blow whistles to each other through the night to communicate that all was safe.

and identified by insomnia – and sometimes even more than a little proud of their wretched wakefulness.

The poet awake while others sleep confronts his or her loneliness in a world askew, with an intensified, at times almost hallucinatory visual and aural acuity. An interior, fun-house array of mirrors furnishes many of these poems, as their wakeful speakers search rooms and windows and looking glasses for some remnant of another, or of a self.[158]

In "Visions of Johanna" we find that theme so common to insomnia poetry of the wakeful writer, the search through rooms and windows and looking glasses (in this case binoculars – "Oh, jewels and binoculars hang from the head of the mule") for a remnant of both another and a self. The song includes the room, the loft, the mirror ("She's delicate and seems like the mirror"), and above all the hallucinatory visual and aural acuity – the visions of Johanna. As much about the hallucinations of the night as about drug experiences, Dylan's song develops brilliantly this tradition of searching for another, and oneself, through the night.

Spaar writes as well about the borderlines between wakefulness and sleep and how important they are to the writer:

---

158   Spaar, L. (ed.)(1999) *Acquainted with the Night. Insomnia Poems.* New York: Columbia University Press, pp. 2-3.

For other poets, the connections between sleeplessness and art, insomnia and poetry, are even more overt and critical. 'There are invisible bridges between sleep and waking.' Octavio Paz has written, and they are crucial to poetry.... Such poets want, as Bernard Spencer writes, to 'sweat the night into words,' with sleeplessness often a metaphor or embodiment of the poem itself.[159]

In her cultural history of insomnia, Summer-Bremmer recounts the ways in which our attitude to sleep and time has changed:

And we tend to be surprised when sleep researchers reveal the variety and extent of the lives we are unknowingly living while we sleep. Our ancestors would not have been surprised by this. To them, sleep was an active part of life whose only distinction from waking activity was that it usually took place in darkness. The gods might visit a sleeper with prophetic dreams, or an enemy take advantage of a hasty slumber....

Insomnia as we know it today was not to be found in the ancient world. The ancients did not have our sense of individual ownership of and beholden-ness to time. Time as a commodity is a modern invention.[160]

---

159   Ibid. p. 13.
160   Summers-Bremmer, E. (2008) *Insomnia: A Cultural History*. London: Reaktion Books, 8, 14.

Proust is a writer fascinated by time and, as another famous insomniac, by the hallucinatory nature of sleeplessness. No surprise that he begins "A la recherché du temps perdu" ("In Remembrance of Times Past") musing on sleep:

> *I would lay my cheeks gently against the comfortable cheeks of my pillow, as plump and blooming as the cheeks of babyhood. Or I would strike a match to look at my watch. Nearly midnight. The hour when an invalid, who has been obliged to start on a journey and to sleep in a strange hotel, awakens in a moment of illness and sees with glad relief a streak of daylight shewing under his bedroom door. Oh, joy of*
>
> *joys! it is morning. The servants will be about in a minute: he can ring, and some one will come to look after him. The thought of being made comfortable gives him strength to endure his pain. He is certain he heard footsteps: they come nearer, and then die away. The ray of light beneath his door is extinguished. It is midnight; some one has turned out the gas; the last servant has gone to bed, and he must lie all night in agony with no one to bring him any help.*

Dylan wrote about the invisible bridge between sleep and waking in another song that dwells on the hallucinatory visual and aural acuity that sleeplessness can bring, and which fits well into the insomnia tradition - "Mr. Tambourine Man":

> *Hey! Mr. Tambourine Man, play a song for me,*
> *I'm not sleepy and there is no place I'm going to.*
>
> *Left me blindly here to stand but still not sleeping.*
> *My weariness amazes me, I'm branded on my feet,*
> *I have no one to meet*
> *And the ancient empty street's too dead for dreaming.*

It's a song that takes us "down the foggy ruins of time" to forgetting about time all together:

> *With all memory and fate driven deep beneath the waves,*
> *Let me forget about today until tomorrow.*

That complex relation between memory and time is something Dylan returns to in "Father of Night", released on "New Morning" in 1970. The Father of night and day is also the father or time, days and minutes:

> *Father of night, Father of day,*
> *Father, who taketh the darkness away....*
>
> *Father of air and Father of trees,*
> *Who dwells in our hearts and our memories,*
> *Father of minutes, Father of days,*
> *Father of whom we most solemnly praise.*

Dylan's interest in time goes beyond insomnia to what it means to waste time, and to the attempt to escape time altogether, which we will look at in the next two sections.

You just kinda wasted......

The "time/mind" rhyme which Dylan uses twice in "Mr Tambourine Man" is a rhyme he and many other have used. It's a lazy rhyme but nonetheless Dylan uses it to good effect in "Don't Think Twice, It's Allright" (released in 1963) where in an endearing, catchy but unkind song he adds a second and final unkindness:

> I ain't sayin' you treated me unkind
> You could have done better but I don't mind
> You just kinda wasted my precious time

As we get wrapped up in the kind/mind/time rhyme, we forget that Dylan has thrown in a second kind in "kinda", which, preceded by "just" is a brilliant resemblance of everyday speech, and which makes us forget for a moment how unkind the end of this song is. The ultimate put-down, it seems, was to be accused of having wasted his time, as that's the line that finishes the song (apart from the song title). And what's so bad about wasting time? Like insomnia, it's kind of a newish idea. Summers-Bremmer comments: "Wasting time first became sinful in the West in the fourteenth century, and in the newly mercantile economy that followed several different kinds of time were in contestable operation. Religious opposition to merchants was based on the fact that lending and borrowing money changed the value of time, to which only God, having created it, could grant meaning."[161]

Wasting time comes up twice more in Dylan's songs in similar vein. In "Fourth Time Around" in 1966 he prefers the "time/mine" rhyme:

> And you, you took me in,
> You loved me then
> You didn't waste time.
> And I, I never took much,
> I never asked for your crutch.
> Now don't ask for mine.

And then again in "Workingman's Blues #2" released in 2006 on "Modern Times", where he returns again to time and memory:

> Now they worry and they hurry and they fuss and they fret
> They waste your nights and days
> Them I will forget
> But you I'll remember always
> Old memories of you to me have clung
> You've wounded me with words

In the first chapter of this book I made a claim that "Blonde on Blonde" is an existential album, and no more so than in its attitude to wasting time and waiting. Time is another thematic element – like love and

161   Summers-Bremmer, E. (2008) *Insomnia: A Cultural History*. London: Reaktion Books, 10.

sex – that structures the album and gives it its intense power. Like many philosophical movements, existentialism was concerned with trying to understand time. Camus' existentialist novel, "The Plague" (existentialism for dummies?), first published in 1947, is *the* story about wasting time. Early in the novel we encounter Jean Tarrou, who has come to the town of the plague, Oran, a few weeks before its onset, but with no seeming purpose for being there.

In a sweet meta-fictional move, the novel's narrator quotes from Tarrou's diaries:

> *These are the only passages in which our visitor's record, at this period, strikes a seemingly personal note. Its significance and the earnestness behind it might escape the reader, on a casual perusal. For example, after describing how the discovery of a dead rat led the hotel cashier to make an error in his bill, Tarrou added: 'Query: How contrive not to waste one's time? Answer: By being fully aware of it all the while. Ways in which this can be done: By spending one's days on an uneasy chair in a dentist's waiting room; by remaining on one's balcony all a Sunday afternoon; by listening to lectures in a language one doesn't know; by travelling by the longest and least convenient train routes, and of course standing all the way; by queuing at the box-office of theatres and not booking a seat. And so forth.'*

Camus realized the importance of staring down the absurd meaningless of existence (if there is no God and no salvation) but recognising and transcending that meaningless, through creation and community. It's a common theme of modern literature, waiting for something, perhaps Godot in Beckett's play:

> *Pozzo: (suddenly furious.) Have you not done tormenting me with your accursed time! It's abominable! When! When! One day, is that not enough for you, one day he went dumb, one day I went blind, one day we'll go deaf, one day we were born, one day we shall die, the same day, the same second, is that not enough for you?*

Another character in "Waiting for Godot", says: "But habit is a great deadener" – Beckett's equivalent of being bored to death, perhaps – and how is it that boredom and death came to be so closely related?

And so that that fate doesn't fall to my intrepid reader, let's move on with no further waiting to "Blonde on Blonde". It's an album where waiting and repetition are central. We have already explored the use of waiting on "Blonde on Blonde" in relation to the "wait/gate" rhyme. But what is it that Dylan is waiting for? Among other things, "Stuck Inside of Mobile with the Memphis Blues Again" is a song about ....being stuck.

> *The ladies treat me kindly*
> *And furnish me with tape*

But deep inside my heart
I know I can't escape

Escape from what, exactly? Perhaps from the weird nonsensical world of the song?

Now the rainman gave me two cures
Then he said, "Jump right in"
The one was Texas medicine
The other was just railroad gin
An' like a fool I mixed them
An' it strangled up my mind
An' now people just get uglier
An' I have no sense of time

No sense of time? What would having a sense of time be like?

In extraordinarily economical language, among my favourite Dylan stanzas, he sings later in the song:

Now the bricks lay on Grand Street
Where the neon madmen climb
They all fall there so perfectly
It all seems so well timed
An' here I sit so patiently
Waiting to find out what price
You have to pay to get out of
Going through all these things twice

More waiting, this time to find out the cost of not doing everything twice in a world where everything is so well timed. Can this really be the end, Dylan asks in the chorus and not quite the end of the song? Not if everything has to be done twice. And one last twist in this song, in the chorus Dylan rhymes end and again, so is this one of those songs where you finish just to start all over again?

Oh, Mama, can this really be the end
To be stuck inside of Mobile
With the Memphis blues again

That feeling of not being able to escape is one that pervades the album. In "Visions of Johanna" they sit stranded: "We sit here stranded though we're all doing our best to deny it." In a song about pledging time, "Pledging my Time":

This room is so stuffy
I can hardly breathe
Everybody's gone but me and you
And I can't be the last to leave

Then there's all that interest in time and all that waiting – waiting in the frozen traffic on "Absolutely Sweet Marie", wondering whether to wait at the end of "Sad-Eyed Lady of the Lowlands" (where every verse ends with waiting, and meaning that the album ends with the word "wait"), waiting while wanting on "I Want You" where he is waiting for the saviours, who are waiting for the women he wants, to interrupt him (and perhaps someone should inform Dylan that you can't wait for someone to interrupt, because interrupting is unexpected; nice rhyme though – interrupt/cup):

> And the saviors who are fast asleep, they wait for you
> And I wait for them to interrupt
> Me drinkin' from my broken cup
> And ask me to
> Open up the gate for you

Who is he pledging his time to on "Pledging My Time"? Why is time on the side of the dancing child in the Chinese suit in "I Want You"? Why did someone in "4th Time Around" never waste his time, and why is it the 4th Time Around (what happened the other three times around)? As Dylan wrote on another song on "Blonde on Blonde" – "Most Likely You Go Your Way (And I'll go mine)" – "Time will tell who has fell/And who's been left behind". Perhaps it will, but we'll leave "Blonde on Blonde" behind and move on from waiting to a new, timeless project - on stopping time.

Making promises by the hours

Using the creative act as a means of moving beyond time into the realm of the eternal moment is a spiritual dream cherished by many modern writers (and drug users). Polito muses on influences on Dylan and Dylan's dealing with time and memory, and quotes Dylan's famous comments on time and "Blood on the Tracks":

Dylan, too, as far back as his Renaldo and Clara pressed the eternising powers of art. "The movie creates and holds the time," he told Jonathan Cott. "That's what it should do – it should hold that time, breathe in that time and stop time in doing that." Or, as he again sketched Blood on the Tracks, "Everybody agrees that was pretty different, and what's different about it is that there's a code in the lyrics and also there's no sense of time. There's no respect for it: you've got yesterday, today and tomorrow all in the same room, and there's little that you can't imagine not happening.[162]

"'Songs are just thoughts," Bob Dylan told Bill Flanagan in 1985. " For the moment they stop time. Songs are supposed to be heroic enough to give the illusion of stopping time."[163] Dylan likewise told Allen Ginsberg in an interview about Renaldo and Clara[164]:

"You wanna stop time, that's what you want to do...In order to stop time you have to exist in the moment, so strong as to stop time and prove your point."

---

162   Polito, R. (2009) "Bob Dylan's Memory Palace." In Sheehy, C. and T. Swiss (eds) *Highway 61 Revisited. Bob Dylan's Road from Minnesota to the World.* Minneapolis: University of Minneapolis Press, 151.
163   Quoted in Williams, P. Bob Dylan. *Mind out of Time (Performing Artist Vol. 3, 1987-2000).* Entwhistle Books, p. 26.
164   Quoted in M. Denning (2009) "Bob Dylan and Rolling Thunder" in Kevin   Dettmar (ed) *The Cambridge Companion to Bob Dylan.* Cambridge: Cambridge University Press, p. 29.

Scobie comments on this period of Dylan's writing:

> In the 1970s, when he was studying painting with Norman Raeben and working on his film *Renaldo and Clara*, Dylan repeatedly said that his aim was to "to stop time". That is, within the bounds of media that absolutely depend on temporal progression (music, film), he paradoxically sought after an ideal of stasis, of spatially arranged simultaneity, that sets up a counterforce to the very movement of the medium itself. Even his idiosyncratic guitar solos, which tend to reiterate single notes rather than extend into melodic lines, may be seen as a variation on this compulsion.[165]

One common way in which Dylan tries to take us outside of time is to compare "short" time and "long" time, yesterday, and eternity. It's a technique he's used since his early writing, for example "Song To Woody", released on his first album in 1962, where, as noted, there is a typical contrast between "tomorrow/today" and "someday":

> I'm leaving tomorrow but I could leave today
> Somewhere down the road someday

There are many songs where he uses this technique – for example the distinction between time and tomorrow in "Oh Sister" from the 1976 album "Desire":

---

[165]   p. 97

Oh sister when I come to knock on your door
Don't turn away, you'll create sorrow
Time is an ocean but it ends at the shore
You may not see me tomorrow

Or a line from "Nettie Moore":

A lifetime with you is like some heavenly day

Or another which reverses the short and long time periods but has the same meaning (from "Things Have Changed"):

The next sixty seconds could be like an eternity

How about riding with someone in a taxi for a mile and half but seeming like it takes forever – a feeling most of us have experienced from a negative perspective, being caught with someone from whom we couldn't wait to escape ("Lenny Bruce" from "Shot of Love" in 1981):

I rode with him in a taxi once, only for a mile and half,
Seemed like it took a couple of months

And how about people you only meet once but remember forever, in "I'll Remember You" from "Empire Burlesque" (1985):

There's some people that
You don't forget,
Even though you've only seen'm
One time or two.

And most sadly of all in perhaps Dylan's saddest song (which is a lot to say about someone who writes so exquisitely about sorrow) "Most of the Time", when the past surprises us with an unbearable moment which stops time in the wrong kind of way:

> I can survive, I can endure
> And I don't even think about her
> Most of the time

Ricks writes about this song[166]:

> What is painful in the song, in its comprehension of pain, is how hideously much must be being conceded, all the way through, with those words 'most of the time'. For the admission within 'most of the time' is that some of the time – perhaps even much of the time – he is not clear focused....and can't keep both feet on the ground, or follow the path, or stay right with it, or handle whatever he stumbles upon.

But the way Dylan brings us to this pain is his typical contrast between long and short time – in the former, he survives and endures, but in the latter, he burns.

Killing time

Let's explore further this theme of trying through art to reach that still point of the turning world, what

---

166   p. 357.

Van Morrison calls the eternal now, that point where time the enemy collapses and is overpowered by the creative present. Past, present, and future become one, when, as Van Morrison repeats in his 2009 repeat of "Astral Weeks", he feels like he is transcending time.

T.S. Eliot dealt with this theme of transcending time in his later poetry, particularly in "Four Quartets" where repetition of phrases in various modes is integral to the structure of the poem, particularly "time past" and "time present" and "end" and "beginning"

Time present and time past
Are both perhaps present in time future,
And time future contained in time past.

Time past and time future
What might have been and what has been
Point to one end, which is always present.

The central theme of "Four Quartets" is to stop time and move to an eternal present, a lifetime burning in every moment - "The still point of the turning world". "Still" is a key poetic word here to which we will return shortly (sic):

Time present and time past
Are both perhaps present in time future
And time future contained in time past.
If all time is eternally present
All time is unredeemable.

As Gish comments: "Although the timeless moment is the idea behind the entire work, its structure is determined by movement towards the meaning of that moment. If the timeless moment is recurrently evoked, the discursive passages consider its meaning for temporal life." [167] "

Eliot's poem, while brilliantly phrased, is not particularly original, for the coming together of past, present and future to stop time is a common poetic and religious theme related to epiphanizing. Polito quotes Spence who quotes Augustine: "In *The Memory Palace of Matteo Ricci*, Spence quotes Augustine from the *Confessions*: 'Perchance it might be properly said: "there be three times; a present of things past, a present of things present, and a present of things future."[168] Petrarch (whom Dylan may have been referring to in "Tangled Up in Blue" when writing about an Italian poet of the 13th century – although he claimed it was Plutarch at one point!) wrote in his poem about the death of time "Triumph of Eternity":

> *Greatly I marveled, seeing time itself*
> *Come to an end, that ne' er before had ceased,*
> *But had been wont in its course to change all things.*
> *Past, present, future: these I saw combined*
> *In a single term, and that unchangeable.*

---

167   Gish, N. (1981) *Time in the Poetry of T.S. Eliot. A Study in Structure and Theme.* New Jersey: Barnes and Noble Books, 96.
168   Polito, p. 151.

Tennyson in a fragment from which Dylan may have borrowed in "When the Deal Goes Down" ("We live and we die, we know not why/.... I laugh and I cry and I'm haunted by/

Things I never meant nor wished to say") similarly and in a lighter vein perhaps wrote in The "How" and the "Why"

> In time there is no present,
> In eternity no future,
> In eternity no past.
> We laugh, we cry, we are born, we die,
> Who will riddle me the how and the why?

Stephen Daedalus provides us with a similar image in "Ulysses" in the scene in the National Library: "that which I was is that which I am and that which in possibility I may come to be. So in the future, the sister of the past, I may see myself as I sit here now but by reflection from that which then I shall be."

Stevens does something similar in "Martial Cadenza":

> It was like sudden time in a world without time,
> This world, this place, the street in which I was,
> Without time: as that which is not has no time....

This too is the religious experience, in that communion with a higher being will take us away from our earthly constraints, or all time is pre-destined, as in "Pressing On", released on "Saved" in 1980:

*What kind of sign they need when it all come
from within
When what's lost has been found, what's to
come has already been?*

In his study of time in literature, Meyerhoff notes several authors who have experienced similar concentrations of time:

> *As De Quincey confessed under the influence of
> drugs: ''The sense of space and, in the end, the
> sense of time were both powerfully affected...
> Sometimes, I seemed to have lived a hundred
> years in one night; nay sometimes had feelings
> of duration far beyond the limits of any human
> experience.".....Thus Proust could write: "A single
> minute released from the chronological order of
> time has re-created in us the human being similarly
> released." ... Or Proust could say: "All the
> memories following one after another were condensed
> into a single substance."[169]*

We are familiar with Dylan's take on "a lifetime burning in every moment", in "Every Grain of Sand" (released on "Shot of Love" in 1981):

> *In the fury of the moment I can see the Master's
> hand
> In every leaf that trembles, in every grain of sand*

---

169   pp. 25, 49-50.

Itself a rediscovery of Blake's famous lines from "Auguries of Innocence":

To see a world in a grain of sand,
And a heaven in a wild flower,
Hold infinity in the palm of your hand,
And eternity in an hour.

In Blake not only time but also time and space come together. Dylan likes to play time and space off against each other, because to do so perhaps means reaching that timeless moment, as in the timeless "One Too many Mornings" (released in 1964) where we hear about the daytime getting dark and the night falling, and this concentration of space and time:

One too many mornings
And a thousand miles behind

In Proust too the search for the eternal moment in the first volume of "In Rememberance of Times Past" with the epiphanies related to taste and movement, most famously the moment where tasting a madeleine sends the narrator into the literary equivalent of a religious rapture which takes him back to a forgotten past:

And so it is with our own past. It is a labour in vain to attempt to recapture it: all the efforts of our intellect must prove futile. The past is hidden somewhere outside the realm, beyond the reach of intellect, in some material object (in the sensation which that material object will give us) which we do not suspect. And as for that object, it depends on chance whether we come upon it or not before we ourselves must die.

...No sooner had the warm liquid, and the crumbs with it, touched my palate than a shudder ran through my whole body, and I stopped, intent upon the extraordinary changes that were taking place. An exquisite pleasure had invaded my senses, but individual, detached, with no suggestion of its origin. And at once the vicissitudes of life had become indifferent to me, its disasters innocuous, its brevity illusory—this new sensation having had on me the effect which love has of filling me with a precious essence; or rather this essence was not in me, it was myself. I had ceased now to feel mediocre, accidental, mortal.... And suddenly the memory returns.[170]

The quest for that moment is typical of romantic poets who strove to go beyond human experience of time. Dylan's circular song "Lay Down Your Weary Tune" operates in this way, as Scobie has said: "The song's dominant feeling is of a moment suspended in time, the moment of the mystic caught up in the rapture of his vision."[171] It's no coincidence that this song also contains the natural imagery much

---

170   On ephiphanies in Proust, see Kearney, R. (2005) "Ephiphanies in Joyce and Proust." *New Arcadia Review*, 3.
171   p. 128.

loved by the romantic poets, because it was often communion with the natural world that led to their own raptures.

Polito writes about Dylan writing about "The Great Gatsby", a novel that dwells on two of Dylan's favourite themes, love and memory:

> *Without ever winking, Dylan proves canny and sophisticated about all this, though after a fashion that recalls Laurence Sterne's celebrated attack on plagiarism, itself plagiarized from The Anatomy of Melancholy. On "Summer Days" from " 'Love and Theft' " Dylan sings:*
>
> *She's looking into my eyes, she's holding my hand*
> *She's looking into my eyes, she's holding my hand*
> *She says, "You can't repeat the past." I say, "You can't? What do you mean, you can't? Of course you can."* [172]

Is her hair still red?

And so back to "Blood on the Tracks", which as usual is guilty of reflecting Dylan's most condensed versions of the common poetic denominators he uses. We saw Dylan's quote that it was in "Blood on the Tracks" where there's no respect for time and you've got "yesterday, today and tomorrow all in

---

172   Polito, p. 150, 153.

the same room." The listeners to whom Dylan first played some songs from the album were stunned by the imagery and couldn't keep up with the images and stream of words.[173] What is striking is the simple language, the one syllable words that dominate, the constantly repeated themes and allusions to other songs on the album, like ballads. It isn't until we get to "Idiot Wind" that there's even a break for a chorus, and even there the chorus doesn't repeat itself as in so many songs but is different each time. As Hedin has noted writing about "Shelter from the Storm": "Like most songs on that album, the lyrics are supported by a hypnotic use of repetition. A single bar of music, built on the three major chords in the key of E, is played over and over beneath the melody, with bass as the only other form of accompaniment."[174] 'Blood on the Tracks" is above all else an album about repeating and trying to transcend the past.

The album's signature tune, "Tangled Up in Blue" sets the tone for that timeless feeling the album evinces. Here, again, are the opening lines:

> *Early one mornin' the sun was shinin',*
> *I was layin' in bed*
> *Wond'rin' if she'd changed at all*
> *If her hair was still red.*

---

173   A. Gill and K. Odegard (2004) *A Simple Twist of Fate: Bob Dylan and the Making of Blood on the Tracks*, De Capo Press.
174   p. 113.

What colour would he expect it to be, and why, considering he is looking back over the past, would he think that she would stay the same? In the notebook where Dylan wrote the lyrics for "Blood on the Tracks", the original opening of the song was:

Five in the mornin' the sun was shinin'

That change to the non-specific "Early one mornin'" introduces the timeless element of the album as well as the reference to the folk ballad of the same name discussed in chapter 4. This vague reference to time outside of clock time continues throughout the song – splitting up on a dark sad night, and meeting again "someday" in the second verse, the use of "never" throughout ("Never did like Mama's homemade dress"; "I never did like it all that much"; "she never escaped my mind"; "I thought you'd never say hello")[175]; and a few other references such as "soon", "finally", "later on" and "always" add to the sense of timelessness. Dylan accentuated the timelessness of the song by including only one reference to actual time: the thirteenth century. As we saw in the last chapter, the song too returns to where it started with the repeated key words in the first and last verse – lives, stillness and the road.

---

175   The chorus to the folk ballad "Early One Morning" is "Oh don't deceive me, Oh *never* leave me, How could you use a poor maiden so?"

As with many of Dylan's references to time, there are two types of time in this song, one that is close by, and one that is distant. For example in the third verse:

> I had a job in the great north woods
> Working as a cook for a spell
> But I never did like it all that much
> And one day the ax just fell.
> So I drifted down to New Orleans
> Where I happened to be employed
> Workin' for a while on a fishin' boat
> Right outside of Delacroix.
> But all the while I was alone
> The past was close behind,
> I seen a lot of women
> But she never escaped my mind, and I just grew
> Tangled up in blue.

What a difference too between 'for a spell' and 'for a while', which refer to immediate time, and 'all the while', which refers to time that goes on and on; and what a difference too between the two uses of 'never', the first again referring to immediate time, and the second to something that will never stop. Together these bring into contrast the pointlessness of the temporal and timelessness that has to be endured.

Dylan uses this short time/long time contrast again on "Idiot Wind", one of the codes that structures the album:

*People see me all the time and they just can't
remember how to act
Their minds are filled with big ideas, images and
distorted facts.
Even you, yesterday you had to ask me where it
was at,
I couldn't believe after all these years, you didn't
know me better than that
Sweet lady.*

The past is creeping close behind in many of the songs on "Blood on the Tracks" as the singer wrestles with his memory. That sense of timelessness continues with "Simple Twist of Fate" which like "Tangled up in Blue" starts in vagueness city:

*They sat together in the park
As the evening sky grew dark*

And later in the same verse "Twas *then* he felt alone.", and in the second verse "He felt the heat of the *night*." In the penultimate verse we return to that sense of endless waiting epitomised by the ticking clocks:

*He hears the ticking of the clocks
And walks along with a parrot that talks,
Hunts her down by the waterfront docks where
the sailors all come in.
Maybe she'll pick him out again, how long must
he wait
Once more for a simple twist of fate.*

How long indeed? Rather than being a throw-away line, "He hears the ticking of the clocks" makes up part of the theme of regretting the past. Ticking clocks, as in "Love Sick" from "Time Out Of Mind" (1997) - "I'm sick of love; I hear the clock tick/

This kind of love; I'm love sick" - reminds us of the seconds and minutes and hours of love lost. It's the pain that stops and starts from "You're a Big Girl Now", which dominates the album. Perhaps he has to wait forever if we take the mysterious last lines of "Simple Twist of Fate" at face value:

> *She was born in spring, but I was born too late*
> *Blame it on a simple twist of fate.*

There are a number of other references to a vague notion of time on the album which help structure it and give it its sense of timelessness - never realizing the time ("You're Going to Make Me Lonesome When You Go"), the darkest hour being right before the dawn ("Meet Me in the Morning"), replaying the past ("If You See Her, Say Hello"), time being like a jet plane ("You're a Big Girl Now"), beginning on a long-forgotten morn ("Shelter from the Storm"), and the springtime turning slowly into autumn ("Idiot Wind")[176].

---

176   In the outtake version of the song Dylan sings: "I've never seen the springtime turn so quickly into autumn" suggesting that what was most important on the song was the generality of the seasons rather than how they changed. In 1976 Dylan sang various versions of "If You See Her, Say Hello", including one with the couplet: "You might say that I'm in disarray and for me time's standing still/ Oh I've never gotten over her, I don't think I ever will."

But perhaps most interesting in terms of timelessness is "Shelter from the Storm", the song with the hypnotic melody. The song's starting point is an unknown time and place:

> Twas in another lifetime, one of toil and blood
> When blackness was a virtue and the road was full of mud
> I came in from the wilderness, a creature void of form.

And ends with a return to something which will happen "someday":

> Well, I'm livin' in a foreign country but I'm bound to cross the line
> Beauty walks a razor's edge, someday I'll make it mine.
> If I could only turn back the clock to when God and her were born.

When he wrote these lines Dylan may have been thinking about the alternate ending to "Idiot Wind" in his notebooks already quoted in chapter 2, as he clearly had God and time on his mind:

> We could change the world with space and time
> Space is place and God is love
> And time is money[177]

---

177   Dylan might have been thinking about the opening to Marvell's "To His Coy Mistress" a poem where time is a third actor, or

He had made the same connection between love, time and money a year earlier in "Wedding Song" from "Planet Waves" (1974):

> *I love you more than ever, more than time and more than love*
> *I love you more than money and more than the stars above*

The final verse of "Shelter from the Storm" also takes us back to "she was born in spring" in "Simple Twist of Fate", but the reference to being born also returns us to "steel-eyed death" earlier in the song, because birth and death are intimately connected in Dylan's conceptions of time. But before we move on to death (and birth) in the last section of this chapter, let's meditate for a few moments on the idea of moving beyond time.

In her chapter on eternity and conceptions of time in the Middle Ages, Bianchi comments that at that time God was conceived as living in an eternal present: [178]

---

perhaps this is just two writers dwelling on the common theme of *carpe diem*:

    Had we but world enough, and time,
    This coyness, lady, were no crime....

    But at my back I always hear
    Time's winged chariot hurrying near;
    And yonder all before us lie
    Deserts of vast eternity.

178   Bianchi, L. (2001) "Abiding Then: Eternity of God and Eternity of The World from Hobbes to the Encyclopedie" In Porro, P. (ed) *The*

> In other words, the infinity arguments in favour of a beginning of the universe could be analysed so scrupulously and unbiasedly because most (though not all) Scholastics argued that God's duration is exempt from any succession: maintaining with Boethius that God lives in an eternal present, in an abiding now (nunc stans), late medieval thinkers were assured that those arguments were valid – if at all – only against the eternity of the creatures, and not against the eternity of the Creator.

But the idea that time could be transcended, the aim of so many artists, did meet with some scepticism, for example Bianchi quotes Hobbes:

> I know St. Thomas Aquinas calls eternity, nunc stans, an ever-abiding now; which is easy enough to say, but though I fain would, yet I could never conceive it: they that can, are more happy than I.

Dylan of course never transcended time, but we have, at least temporarily, been brought to that ever-biding now by the power of his songs, and away from our obsessions with time and money.

May you stay forever young: stillness and death

Dylan has been writing and singing about death from the beginning of his career, because the Blues singers from whom he borrowed in the late 1950s

---

Medieval Concept of Time, Leiden: Brill, 547, 551, 552.

and early 1960s had death on their minds, for example "In My Time of Dyin' ", "Fixin' to Die" and "See That My Grave is Kept Clean" from his first, and melancholy, album, "Bob Dylan", released in 1962.

Aging and death – like love, sex, time, travel and writing – has been a constant preoccupation of modern Western writers, and one that continues to preoccupy Dylan. As one commentator notes, "Dylan's Theme Time Radio Hour is preoccupied with mortality. He seems to take an almost perverse delight in reciting accounts of early deaths, boating and car accidents, plane crashes, alcoholism and cirrhosis, drug overdoses."[179] Recently Dylan has become quite mopey in his songs – as if he hadn't figured out yet that aging for a rock star might not be that much fun! On the other hand, there's an element of resignation on "Time Out Of Mind" (1997), as album which stares down time, death and the impending darkness on several of its tracks, and starts with Dylan's half-dead voice singing:

I'm walking through streets that are dead

W.B. Yeats has an interesting take on aging and, self-mocking, made the old poet a character in his later poetry, for example in "Among School children" which includes the poet at 60:

---

179   Cochrane, M. (2009) "Bob Dylan's Lives of the Poets" in In Sheehy, C. and T. Swiss (eds) *Highway 61 Revisited. Bob Dylan's Road from Minnesota to the World.* Minneapolis: University of Minneapolis Press, 136.

And I though never of Ledaean kind
Had pretty plumage once - enough of that,
Better to smile on all that smile, and show
There is a comfortable kind of old scarecrow.

World-famous golden-thighed Pythagoras
Fingered upon a fiddle-stick or strings
What a star sang and careless Muses heard:
Old clothes upon old sticks to scare a bird.

And in "Sailing to Byzantium", also published when Yeats was 60:

An aged man is but a paltry thing,
A tattered coat upon a stick, unless
Soul clap its hands and sing, and louder sing
For every tatter in its mortal dress.

The release from age through soul clapping its hands and singing is largely absent from Dylan. And Dylan is not immune to a little self-pity– this from "Highlands" released in "Time Out Of Mind" – a little boy lost who likes to brag of his misery?:

Feel like a prisoner in a world of mystery
I wish someone would come
And push back the clock for me

I see people in the park forgetting their troubles and woes
They're drinking and dancing, wearing bright colored clothes

All the young men with their young women look-
ing so good
Well, I'd trade places with any of them
In a minute, if I could

The ending of "Bye and Bye" is similarly sanguine, suggesting the interchangeability of time as well as its completion - "Well the future for me is already a thing of the past".

Old Man Dylan is also not immune to a little self-aggrandizement, as in "Spirit on the Water" from "Modern Times" (2006):

You think I'm over the hill
You think I'm past my prime
Let me see what you got
We can have a whoppin' good time

Birth and death are often bound together in his songs, to emphasize the pointlessness of living, as in "It's AlRight, Ma (I'm Only Bleeding)" (released in 1964):

The hollow horn plays wasted words
Proves to warn
That he not busy being born
Is busy dying.

Or in the opposite order in the bleak "North Country Blues" (released in 1963):

There's seven people dead on a South Dakota farm
There's seven people dead on a South Dakota farm
Somewhere's in the distance there's seven new people born

There are also references, as might be anticipated, in Dylan's religious songs, demonstrating again that certain themes structure his work from start to finish. Here is one example from "What Can I Do For You?", from the 1980 album "Saved":

Soon as a man is born, you know the sparks begin to fly,
He gets wise in his own eyes and he's made to believe a lie.
Who would deliver him from the death he's bound to die?

Other references to life, birth and death are equally contemplative, as in "When the Deal Goes Down" from the 2006 "Modern Times". In this song Dylan uses his favourite technique comparing "tomorrow" to life and death in an effort to transcend the former "short" time, and writes with resignation about the certainty of dying and the need to grasp onto things we value:

Tomorrow keeps turning around
We live and we die, we know not why
But I'll be with you when the deal goes down

More complex is the puzzling "Oh Sister" from "Desire" (1976). Few commentators on Dylan have written about this beautiful and mysterious song, and it seems out of place on "Desire" and its focus on gangsters, imprisoned boxers and impassioned love. On the album cover Dylan wrote:

> oh sister, when I fall into your spacy arms, can not ya feel the weight of oblivion and the songs of redemption on your backside

Dylan doesn't expand on the how heavy oblivion is, or what the songs of redemption feel like, but he does write about – perhaps religious – death and rebirth.

> We grew up together
> From the cradle to the grave
> We died and were reborn
> And then mysteriously saved.

Talking of themes structuring his work, here is the same theme in the early "Song to Woody" (1962):

> Hey, hey Woody Guthrie, I wrote you a song
> 'Bout a funny ol' world that's a-comin' along.
> Seems sick an' it's hungry, it's tired an' it's torn,
> It looks like it's a-dyin' an' it's hardly been born.

And birth and death are together again on "Not Dark Yet" (1997), Dylan's brilliant and haunting ode to the approaching blackness:

I was born here and I'll die here against my will
*I know it looks like I'm moving, but I'm standing
still*
Every nerve in my body is so vacant and numb
*I can't even remember what it was I came here
to get away from*
Don't even hear a murmur of a prayer
It's not dark yet, but it's getting there.

Me I'm still on the road

Dylan's not alone in living and dying here against his will, it happens to most of us. But is there the murmur of a prayer in the way he uses the word "still"? A favourite word of many poets, because still is a word that means its opposite: as an adverb it means both constant movement, and without movement[180]; and has a third poetic meaning as a noun, which is "tranquil silence".

In Chapter 4 we've already looked at the way Dylan uses "still" in "Tangled Up in Blue":

But me, I'm still on the road
Headin' for another joint
We always did feel the same,
We just saw it from a different point of view

---

180   The Oxford English Dictionary defines still as: (adjective) "not moving or making a sound" (adverb) "up to and including the present or the time mentioned: even now (or then) as formerly."

Meaning perhaps that he is both moving on the road, and in stasis on the road. Is there the same meaning in "Not Dark Yet" – the singer is both standing motionless, but still standing despite all that has happened?

"Still" was a key word, and perhaps the central word, for T.S. Eliot in "Four Quartets", because the "still point of the turning world" is the still point about which the poem revolves:

> At the still point of the turning world. Neither flesh nor fleshless;
> Neither from nor towards; at the still point, there the dance is,
> But neither arrest nor movement. And do not call it fixity,
> Where past and future are gathered. Neither movement from nor towards,
> Neither ascent nor decline. Except for the point, the still point,
> There would be no dance, and there is only the dance.

Eliot returns to stillness throughout, including when reflecting on age and exploration at the end of the second of the four quartets, "East Coker":

> Old men ought to be explorers
> Here or there does not matter
> We must be still and still moving
> Into another intensity
> For a further union, a deeper communion

In her comparative study of the use of the concept of eternity in Blake and Yeats, Billigheimer comments on Yeats' poetry: "Throughout the poetry of Yeats there is a tension of opposing forces, life and death, youthful love and old age, and movement and stillness. The predominant concern is with time and eternity and their inter-relationship."[181] We might make a similar claim for some of Dylan's work – time, death, movement and stillness are all poetic themes that have structured his work since its origins. And would it be too far out to suggest that when he finished the first song of that album of movement and stasis – "Blood on the Tracks" – a song that starts with the singer meditatively lying in bed and ends with him still on the road – he had in the back of his mind the stillness and the point from Eliot's "Still point of the turning world"?:

> But me, I'm still on the road
> Headin' for another joint
> We always did feel the same,
> We just saw it from a different point of view

This is just about the end of the book, intrepid reader. We have covered much ground, looking at some of the central themes which structure Dylan's work and bind it into a coherent whole – love, sex and money; writing; the highway; time and death. We have attempted to understand the power of

---

181   Billigheimer, R. (1990) *Wheels of Eternity. A Comparative Study of William Blake and William Butler Yeats.* New York: St. Martin's Press, 99.

Dylan's lyrics through the ways in which he has used common poetic denominators that have been central to modern western literature. In this book, I hope I haven't made too many promises by the hours, and have kept you trapped by no track of hours because they hang suspended. I'll end with the line from "All Along The Watchtower" with which Dylan closes many concerts these days (not the end of the song, but Dylan's final end):

So let us not talk falsely now, the hour is getting late.

Acknowledgements for copyright

Thanks are due for the following permissions to use copyrighted material. Any quotes that are not included below have been included under "fair use" guidelines provided by the publishers.

Bob Dylan songs

Talking New York. Copyright © 1962, 1965 by Duchess Music Corporation; renewed 1990, 1993 by MCA
Song to Woody. Copyright © 1962, 1965 by Duchess Music Corporation; renewed 1990, 1993 by MCA
Girl from the North Country. Copyright © 1963 by Warner Bros. Inc.; renewed 1991 by Special Rider Music
Blowin' in the Wind. Copyright © 1962 by Warner Bros. Inc.; renewed 1990 by Special Rider Music
Oxford Town. Copyright © 1963 by Warner Bros. Inc.; renewed 1992 by Special Rider Music
A Hard Rain's A-gonna Fall. Copyright © 1963 by Warner Bros. Inc.; renewed 1991 by Special Rider Music
I Shall Be Free. Copyright © 1963, 1967 by Warner Bros. Inc.; renewed 1991, 1995 by Special Rider Music

Gates of Eden. Copyright © 1965 by Warner Bros. Inc.; renewed 1993 by Special Rider Music

It's Alright Ma (I'm Only Bleeding). Copyright © 1965 by Warner Bros. Inc.; renewed 1993 by Special Rider Music

Mr. Tambourine Man. Copyright © 1964, 1965 by Warner Bros. Inc.; renewed 1992, 1993 by Special Rider Music

It Takes a Lot to Laugh, It Takes a Train to Cry. Copyright © 1965 by Warner Bros. Inc.; renewed 1993 by Special Rider Music

Like a Rolling Stone. Copyright © 1965 by Warner Bros. Inc.; renewed 1993 by Special Rider Music

Just Like Tom Thumb's Blues. Copyright © 1965 by Warner Bros. Inc.; renewed 1993 by Special Rider Music

Desolation Row. Copyright © 1965 by Warner Bros. Inc.; renewed 1993 by Special Rider Music

Ballad of a Thin Man. Copyright © 1965 by Warner Bros. Inc.; renewed 1993 by Special Rider Music

Tombstone Blues. Copyright © 1965 by Warner Bros. Inc.; renewed 1993 by Special Rider Music

Rainy Day Women #12 & 35. Copyright © 1966 by Dwarf Music; renewed 1994 by Dwarf Music

Pledging My Time. Copyright © 1966 by Dwarf Music; renewed 1994 by Dwarf Music

Visions of Johanna. Copyright © 1966 by Dwarf Music; renewed 1994 by Dwarf Music

One of Us Must Know (Sooner or Later). Copyright © 1966 by Dwarf Music; renewed 1994 by Dwarf Music

I Want You. Copyright © 1966 by Dwarf Music; renewed 1994 by Dwarf Music

Stuck Inside of Mobile with the Memphis Blues Again. Copyright © 1966 by Dwarf Music; renewed 1994 by Dwarf Music

Leopard-Skin Pill-Box Hat. Copyright © 1966 by Dwarf Music; renewed 1994 by Dwarf Music

Most Likely You Go Your Way (And I'll Go Mine). Copyright © 1966 by Dwarf Music; renewed 1994 by Dwarf Music

Temporary Like Achilles. Copyright © 1966 by Dwarf Music; renewed 1994 by Dwarf Music

Absolutely Sweet Marie. Copyright © 1966 by Dwarf Music; renewed 1994 by Dwarf Music

4th Time Around. Copyright © 1966 by Dwarf Music; renewed 1994 by Dwarf Music

Sad-Eyed Lady of the Lowlands. Copyright © 1966 by Dwarf Music; renewed 1994 by Dwarf Music

I Dreamed I Saw St. Augustine. Copyright © 1968 by Dwarf Music; renewed 1996 by Dwarf Music

All Along the Watchtower. Copyright © 1968 by Dwarf Music; renewed 1996 by Dwarf Music

Lay Lady Lay. Copyright © 1969 by Big Sky Music; renewed 1997 by Big Sky Music

Three Angels. Copyright © 1970 by Big Sky Music; renewed 1998 by Big Sky Music

Sign on the Window. Copyright © 1970 by Big Sky Music; renewed 1998 by Big Sky Music

New Morning. Copyright © 1970 by Big Sky Music; renewed 1998 by Big Sky Music

If Not for You. Copyright © 1970 by Big Sky Music; renewed 1998 by Big Sky Music

Father of Night. Copyright © 1970 by Big Sky Music; renewed 1998 by Big Sky Music

I Shall Be Released. Copyright ©1967, 1970 by Dwarf Music; renewed 1995 by Dwarf Music

Watching the River Flow. Copyright © 1971 by Big Sky Music; renewed 1999 by Big Sky Music

You Angel You. Copyright © 1973 by Ram's Horn Music; renewed 2001 by Ram's Horn Music

On a Night Like This. Copyright © 1973 by Ram's Horn Music; renewed 2001 by Ram's Horn Music

Something There is About You. Copyright © 1973 by Ram's Horn Music; renewed 2001 by Ram's Horn Music

Wedding Song. Copyright © 1973 by Ram's Horn Music; renewed 2001 by Ram's Horn Music

Tangled up in Blue. Copyright © 1974 by Ram's Horn Music; renewed 2002 by Ram's Horn Music

Simple Twist of Fate. Copyright © 1974 by Ram's Horn Music; renewed 2002 by Ram's Horn Music

You're a Big Girl Now. Copyright © 1974 by Ram's Horn Music; renewed 2002 by Ram's Horn Music

Idiot Wind. Copyright © 1974 by Ram's Horn Music; renewed 2002 by Ram's Horn Music

Meet Me in the Morning. Copyright © 1974 by Ram's Horn Music; renewed 2002 by Ram's Horn Music

Lily, Rosemary and the Jack of Hearts. Copyright © 1974 by Ram's Horn Music; renewed 202 by Ram's Horn Music

If You See Her Say Hello. Copyright © 1974 by Ram's Horn Music; renewed 2002 by Ram's Horn Music

Shelter from the Storm. Copyright © 1974 by Ram's Horn Music; renewed 2002 by Ram's Horn Music

Million Dollar Bash. Copyright © 1967 by Dwarf Music; renewed 1995 by Dwarf Music

Oh, Sister. Copyright © 1975 by Ram's Horn Music; renewed 2003 by Ram's Horn Music

Joey. Copyright © 1975 by Ram's Horn Music; renewed 2003 by Ram's Horn Music

Sara. Copyright © 1975, 1976 by Ram's Horn Music; renewed 2003, 2004 by Ram's Horn Music

Senor (Tales of Yankee Power). Copyright © 1978 by Special Rider Music

Watching the River Flow. Copyright © 1971 by Big Sky Music; renewed 1999 by Big Sky Music

Precious Angel. Copyright © 1979 by Special Rider Music

I Believe in You. Copyright © 1979 by Special Rider Music

Slow Train. Copyright © 1979 by Special Rider Music

What Can I Do for You?. Copyright © 1980 by Special Rider Music

Shot of Love. Copyright © 1981 by Special Rider Music

Lenny Bruce. Copyright © 1981 by Special Rider Music

Every Grain of Sand. Copyright © 1981 by Special Rider Music

Jokerman. Copyright © 1983 by Special Rider Music

Sweetheart Like You. Copyright © 1983 by Special Rider Music

I and I. Copyright © 1983 by Special Rider Music

Don't Fall Apart on Me Tonight. Copyright © 1983 by Special Rider Music

Dark Eyes. Copyright © 1985 by Special Rider Music

I'll Remember You. Copyright © 1985 by Special Rider Music

Percy's Song. Copyright © 1964, 1966 by Warner Bros. Inc.; renewed 1992, 1994 by Special Rider Music

I'll Keep It with Mine. Copyright © 1965, 1968 by Warner Bros. Inc.; renewed 1993, 1996 by Special Rider Music

Abandoned Love. Copyright © 1975 by Ram's Horn Music; renewed 2003 by Ram's Horn Music

Lay Down Your Weary Tune. Copyright © 1964, 1965 by Warner Bros. Inc.; renewed 1992, 1993 by Special Rider Music

Under Your Spell. Copyright © 1986 by Special Rider Music and Carol Bayer Sager Music

Most of the Time. Copyright © 1989 by Special Rider Music

Ring Them Bells. Copyright © 1989 by Special Rider Music

Man in the Long Black Coat. Copyright © 1989 by Special Rider Music

Everything is Broken. Copyright © 1989 by Special Rider Music

Walls of Red Wing. Copyright © 1963 by Warner Bros. Inc.; renewed 1991 by Special Rider Music

Walkin' Down the Line. Copyright © 1963, 1965 by Warner Bros. Inc.; renewed 1991, 1993 by Special Rider Music

Only a Hobo. Copyright © 1963, 1968 by Warner Bros. Inc.; renewed 1991, 1996 by Special Rider Music

Farewell Angelina . Copyright © 1965, 1966 by Warner Bros. Inc.; renewed 1993, 1994 by Special Rider Music

Eternal Circle. Copyright © 1963, 1964 by Warner Bros. Inc.; renewed 1991, 1992 by Special Rider Music

Blind Willie McTell. Copyright © 1983 by Special Rider Music

Love Henry. Copyright ©1993 Special Rider Music

R. Belknap: excerpts from *The List. The Uses and Pleasures of Cataloguing*. Reprinted by permission of Yale University Press.

D. Boucher: *Dylan and Cohen. Poets of Rock and Roll*. Printed with permission from the Continuum International Publishing Company.

L. Bianchi: *Abiding Then: Eternity of God and Eternity of The World from Hobbes to the Encyclopedie*. Brill, 2001.

C. Ricks: *Dylan's Visions of Sin*. Harper Collins, 2003.

Delany, P., *Literature, Money and the Market: From Trollope to Amis*. 2002. Reproduced with permission of Palgrave Macmillan.

Filene, Benjamin: *Romancing the Folk. Public Memory and American Roots Music*. Reprinted by permission of Chapel Hill, University of North Carolina.

Gish, N., *Time in the Poetry of T.S. Eliot. A Study in Structure and Theme*. 1981. Reproduced with permission of Palgrave Macmillan.

Song and Dance Man III. Printed with permission from the Continuum International Publishing Company. Gray, Michael. © 2002.

H. Meyerhoff: *Time in Literature*. Reprinted by permission of Berkeley: University of California Press.

J. Dunlap: *Through the eyes of Tom Joad: patterns of American idealism, Bob Dylan, and the Folk Protest Movement*. Reprinted by permission of Popular Music and Society.

G. Marcus: *Like a Rolling Stone. Bob Dylan at the Crossroads. An explosion of vision and humor that forever changed pop music*. Reprinted by permission of Faber & Faber Limited.

R. Primeau: *Romance of the Road*. Reprinted with permission of Bowling Green: Bowling Green State University Popular Press.

J. Steinbeck. *Travels with Charley. In Search of America*. Reprinted with permission of The Viking Press.

M.H. Abrams: *The Correspondent Breeze. Essays on English Romanticism*. Reprinted with permission of W.W. Norton.

T. Gilfoyle: *City of Eros. New York City, Prostitution and the Commercialization of Sex*. Reprinted with permission of W.W. Norton.

A. Peyronie: "The Labyrinth" in *Companion to Literary Myths, Heroes and Archetypes*. ed: P. Brunel. Reprinted with permission of Routledge.

J. Lomax & A. Lomax, eds: *Our Singing Country: Folk Songs and Ballads*. Reprinted with permission of Dover.

M. Cochrane: "Bob Dylan's Lives of the Poets" in *Highway 61 Revisited. Bob Dylan's Road from Minnesota to the World*. eds: C. Sheehy & T. Swiss. Reprinted with permission of University of Minneapolis Press.

Fontana, Ernest L.: "Victorian Doors" in *Philosophy and Literature*. Vol. 30. Reprinted with permission of JHU Press.

Masur, Louis. "Famous Long Ago. Bob Dylan Revisited." in *American Quarterly*. Vol. 59. Reprinted with the journals permission.

Excerpt from *Down the Highway*, copyright © 2001 by Howard Sounes. Used by permission of Grove/Atlantic Inc.

Made in the USA
Lexington, KY
24 May 2013